THE BEST YEARS OF THEIR LIVES

A Resource Guide for Teenagers in Crisis

Stephanie Zvirin

AMERICAN LIBRARY ASSOCIATION

Chicago and London 1992

Cover and text design by Harriett Banner

Composed by Interface Studio in Garamond and Helvetica on Compugraphic 9600

Printed on 50-pound Finch Opaque, a pH-neutral stock, and bound in 10 pt.
    C1S by Edwards Brothers, Inc.

The paper used in this publication meets the minimum requirements of American National Standard for Information Sciences—Permanence of Paper for Printed Library Materials, ANSI Z39.48-1984. ∞

Library of Congress Cataloging-in-Publication Data
Zvirin, Stephanie.
    The best years of their lives : a resource guide for teenagers in
crisis / Stephanie Zvirin.
        p.   cm.
    Includes index.
    Summary: A selective, annotated bibliography of fiction and non-
fiction self-help works for teenagers, arranged under such topics as
"Family Matters," "Crack, Glue, or a Six-pack or Two?" and "Sex Stuff."
    ISBN 0-8389-0586-2
    1. Teenagers—Juvenile literature—Bibliography.   2. Adolescent psychology—
Juvenile literature—Bibliography.   3. Children's stories—Bibliography.
4. Children's films—Bibliography. [1. Adolescence—Bibliography.]   I. Title.
Z7164.Y8Z95   1992
[HQ796]
016.30523'5—dc20   92-5575
                                                                                CIP

Printed in the United States of America.

96 95 94   5 4 3 2

To Michael and Bob

Contents

Preface

"NEVER BEFORE has one generation of American teenagers been less healthy, less cared for, or less prepared for life than their parents were at the same age." These harsh words, issued in a 1990 report to the nation on America's teenagers, came from C. Everett Koop, former Surgeon General, and representatives of the National Association of State Boards of Education and the American Medical Association.[1] Their concerns are well founded. Suicide rates among young people have skyrocketed. The Alan Guttmacher Institute in New York tells us that one out of every 10 girls ages 15 to 19 becomes pregnant every year.[2] Sexually transmitted diseases have reached epidemic proportions among teens; the Centers for Disease Control cites syphilis rates at their highest level since World War II, and concern about AIDS is growing.[3] The economic health of the nation is also of import to today's teenagers. Will there be jobs when young adults graduate? The Fordham Institute for Innovations in Social Policy discloses that finding steady work is among teenagers' top ten concerns.[4] More troubling still is the question of whether or not today's youth will even finish school. A 1991 Children's Defense Fund study notes that nearly 29 percent of the teenagers who entered ninth grade in 1984 had failed to graduate four years later, and it foresees no "quick fixes" for the high dropout rate.[5]

Social scientists, medical professionals, and educators are responding to these disquieting revelations in a variety of ways. Adolescent parenting programs are being instituted in schools; day-care centers on a few high school campuses enable teen mothers to complete their educations; health classes are being supplanted by "wellness" curriculums, which incorporate discussion of mental health issues along with information on physiology and general health; and drug-awareness programs and activities are being implemented as early as first grade.

The publishing industry has also reacted. While teenage novels dealing with issues such as alcoholism, sexual abuse, and divorce have an established place in publishers' catalogs and on library and bookstore shelves, nonfiction books about those subjects are relatively new arrivals. Writers often avoided such controversial subjects, in part because their publishers felt market response was uncertain. Even slower to gain acceptance have been practical books that help young adults actively address personal crises in their lives. During the last five years, however, much has changed. "Self-help" nonfiction has come into its own in books for teenagers. Calls for such materials by the educational community, increased publicity about Twelve Step programs used by such organizations as Alcoholics Anonymous, and the demand for adult self-help literature that has swept across the country have contributed to the shift. Today, most publishers of juvenile materials have self-help books on their lists, including some titles for very young children; a few publishers, such as Facts on File and the Rosen Publishing Group, even have their own self-help series, though titles usually vary considerably in quality from book to book.

While such books can be excellent resources for young people seeking a better understanding of the challenges they face and the choices they have, self-help books are not substitutes for professional medical or psychiatric care. Nor do most of their authors, many of whom are medical professionals, suggest that they are. Bibliotherapy, in which a facilitator directs the use of literature (fiction or nonfiction) to promote mental or physical health in the rehabilitative or clinical sense, is the province of specially trained professionals, not the majority of teachers, librarians, or the authors of books. Yet, self-help books can be effective in several ways when used by teenagers dealing with developmental concerns.

1. They provide young adults with a sense of what they have in common with others their age, whether that be an unplanned pregnancy, an abusive parent, or simply pimples on their face.

2. They provide background information and useful suggestions for more confident handling of situations that occur in daily life, such as dating or sharing a room with a brother or sister.

3. They help teenagers determine life choices and adjust to the consequences of decision making.

4. They inform teens about the physical and psychological changes that come with adolescence.

The Best Years of Their Lives is a selective guide to nonfiction, accompanied by an assortment of related fiction and video titles, that can give adolescents, ages 12 to 18, a better understanding of what growing up in a rapidly changing world is all about. With the exception of a few outstanding or unusual titles, most of the material included has been published since 1986 and is currently in print.

Though the motivated middle-class young adult is the intended audience of much self-help material, the subjects dealt with—sexuality, peer pressure, stress, and so on—are of concern to most teenagers. Trade books from major publishers for specific audiences, such as black or Jewish or disabled teenagers, are difficult to find. Small presses have begun to fill the breach, but a lot of what's currently available from them is targeted to the educational community and marketed with workbooks and teachers' guides. These materials have not been evaluated in the selection that follows, which concentrates on readily available books and videos of use to independant readers who want materials germane to their personal interests and needs.

At the opposite end of the spectrum come personal profiles of young adults who have endured or overcome great odds. Many such full-length, inspirational stories are available to teenage readers, though only collective biographies, far fewer in number, have been evaluated in this text. Books in series, a few of which are incorporated in the book list, have been evaluated as single titles and are available separately.

All nonfiction and film annotations contain bibliographic information, content description, and evaluative comments. Plot summaries are provided with fiction listings, which include books by such well-known authors of realistic teen novels as Judy Blume, Richard Peck, Gloria Miklowitz, and Virginia Hamilton. Age-level designations, provided for all entries, are suggestions only. The designations are based on a variety of factors, including subject matter, format, depth of treatment, and the writing style.

Were it not for the support of my colleagues at *Booklist,* this book could not have been written. My special thanks to Sally Estes and Hazel Rochman, friends as well as coworkers, and to my good friend Ellen Mandel, whose film expertise gave the book an important dimension it would otherwise have lacked. Finally, I acknowledge with gratitude Janet Bode, Jill Krementz, Eda LeShan, Lynda Madaras, and Gloria Waity, each of whom took time out of her busy schedule to speak with me.

NOTES

1. Felicity Barringer, "Found: Another Lost Generation. What Is Youth Coming To?" *New York Times* (9 June 1990): 24.
2. Children's Defense Fund, *The State of America's Children: 1991* (Washington, D.C.: Children's Defense Fund, 1991).
3. Barbara Kantrowitz, "The Dangers of Doing It," *Newsweek* CXV no. 27 (June 1990): 56-57.
4. David Gelman, "A Much Riskier Passage," *Newsweek* CXV no. 27 (June 1990): 10-16.
5. Children's Defense Fund, *State of America's Children,* 76.

Family Matters

MARKED NOT ONLY BY sexual maturation, adolescence is a time of changing relationships within the family. Teenagers naturally strive to break away from their parents and assume more responsibility for themselves. As they become more self-confident, their roles at home change. Old ties with their parents are broken and new bonds, based more on shared experience and mutual respect, are formed. The process is often an upsetting one for all concerned, but it is further complicated when a family is divided by divorce or burdened by internal conflicts such as serious sibling rivalry. The books in this chapter explore these special challenges along with other issues that may cause tension within families and between parents and teens.

"My mom's the best mom in the world, whatever she is."
—from *Different Mothers*

NONFICTION

Getting Along with One Another

Bernstein, Joanne E., and Bryna J. Fireside. *Special Parents, Special Children.* 1991. Morton Grove, Ill.: Albert Whitman (0–8075–7559–3). Ages 9–13.

What's it like to live with parents who are physically challenged? Sixth grader Lisa Kavanaugh, seventh grader Angela Stewart, fourth grader Adam Holdsworth, and high school sophomore Stephanie Rigert can tell you. They each have at least one parent who has to cope with a physical limitation. John Kavanaugh is blind; the Stewarts are both deaf; Adam's father cannot walk; and Connie and Bob Rigert are achondroplastic dwarfs. Black-and-white photographs personalize family profiles in which parents describe the discrimination they've experienced and what their daily life is like, while their kids talk about family relationships, personal goals, and the frustrations of living with parents who are different. The terminology is not always "politically correct." For example, Lisa and the authors frequently refer to Mr. Kavanaugh as "blind" rather than "visually impaired." But that won't matter to most readers; what *will* impress them are the strength and optimism that shine through these unusual family portraits.

Blume, Judy. *Letters to Judy: What Your Kids Wish They Could Tell You.* 1986. New York: Putnam (0–399–13129–9); Pocket, paper (0–671–62696–5). Ages 11–up.

Though Blume, a popular writer of children's fiction, aimed this book at parents, her young fans will be just as interested in getting a copy. At its heart are the author's fan letters, sent mostly by middle-school- and junior-high-age children. Blume has organized the letters into ten topical chapters representing a range of young people's concerns, from puberty and popularity to divorce, incest, and other sensitive issues.

Scattered among the chapters are memories of Blume's childhood and her experiences as a parent. Blume includes a salting of homespun advice, but her objective is to supply readers with material for opening parent-child dialogue, not to psychologize. Blume's popularity among young people makes her a spokesperson who will attract kids' attention, and her empathy and candor will endear her to parents.

Bode, Janet. *Truce: Ending the Sibling War.* 1991. New York: Watts (0–531–15221–9). Ages 13–18.

Bode sets aside "routine aggravations" that arise between brothers and sisters to concentrate on problems between siblings that turn homes into battlefields where emotional or physical injury actually occurs.

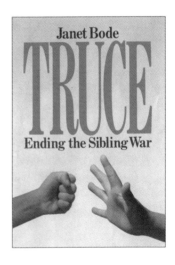

Remarks from family counselors and others who work with the young add authority to the well-documented text, which explores how such factors as birth order, divorce, family coping mechanisms, and poverty influence relationships. The book is not easy to read; personal testimony awkwardly interrupts the narrative. What's more, the family portraits Bode paints are very disturbing; teens recall how they were beaten, sexually abused, or viciously ridiculed by a brother or sister. But Bode tackles aspects of sibling rivalry not often acknowledged, and she offers teens trapped in harmful situations some reasonable strategies to reduce their stress, improve their communication skills, and raise their self-esteem.

"I'd really wanted a brother or sister since I was God knows how old. When it happened for real though, it all happened so quick. I was used to it being just me and my mom, and one morning she got remarried. Then it was me and my mom and my dad—now Xavier and Desmon and then Michael, the baby. . . . I didn't like it." Armando, age 16
—from *Truce*

Cohen, Shari. *Coping with Sibling Rivalry*. 1989. New York: Rosen (0–8239–0977–8). Ages 12–16.

Like Bode in the previously cited book, free-lance writer Cohen also speaks to teens with sibling problems and employs comments from young people and information supplied by professional family counselors to add texture to her discussion. But while Bode concentrates on the most serious kinds of sibling discord, Cohen focuses largely on mundane, widely experienced gripes, such as teasing, borrowing something without asking, or making promises that aren't kept. Without patronizing, she suggests ways readers can cope with these everyday woes, mixing good sense with a generous measure of real compassion.

Different Mothers. Ed. by Louise Rafkin. 1990. San Francisco: Cleis Press (0–939416–40–9). Ages 15–up.

"I am writing this introduction to parents but in my heart I have put together this book for kids," writes Rafkin, who has assembled the frank responses of twenty-seven individuals, many of them teenagers, who've grown up with a lesbian parent. Males and females, ranging in age from 5 to 40, speak frankly. Some remember how their parent "came out" to them or talk about their mother's lesbianism in relation to their own sexual identity; others explain how they feel about being shuttled back and forth between parents who've split up, about keeping mom's lesbianism a secret, or having two "moms" and no dad. In many ways, the words demonstrate to what extent children "carry the burden of social stigma" for having a lesbian parent. Yet they also capture feelings and situations common to most parent-child relationships. It will be these revelations that push readers, especially those with lesbian mothers, beyond stereotype toward recognition of other more important things—about their parent, about affection, and about the nature of families.

Gay, Kathlyn. *The Rainbow Effect: Interracial Families*. 1987. New York: Watts (0–531–10343–9). Ages 12–16.

Gay suggests that teenagers who grow up in interracial or interethnic families are no more apt to have serious identity conflicts than those who do not. While that's good news for kids in such situations, Gay also makes it plain that mixed families still face many challenges. Carefully documenting her material, she explores some of the most significant problems affecting these families, among them prejudice, rejection by extended family members, and community harassment. Interspersed through the text, comments from teenagers add personal dimension to the issues, but Gay is less concerned with individual experience and coping mechanisms than with plain facts. With little teenage material available on this subject, however, her competent text supplies a valuable perspective that kids growing up in interracial families may need to handle their lives more smoothly.

Johnson, Eric W. *How to Live with Parents and Teachers*. 1986. Philadelphia: Westminster (0–664–21273–5). Ages 12–14.

Best known for his straightforward *Love and Sex in Plain Language,* Johnson presents an equally forthright, reassuring book about getting along with adults. Organizing his material into short, alphabetically arranged segments, he considers more than 100 common areas of adult-child confrontation—pets, drug use, and study habits, among them—and offers sensible advice to help young readers deal with conflict and coexist more compatibly with grownups. The book's format promotes browsing, and the brief entries can easily be used to spark discussion in a classroom or between parents and children at home.

LeShan, Eda. *When Grownups Drive You Crazy.* 1988. New York: Macmillan (0–02–756340–5). Ages 10–14.

Like Johnson, LeShan, a child advocate, family counselor, and the author of a number of perceptive books for children, also recognizes the importance of successful adult-child interactions. Her chatty overview considers the relationships between kids and grandparents, teachers, and others with whom young people interact on a regular basis, but its real focus is on what happens between kids and their parents. Using specific examples, the author reveals what's behind many adult behaviors, providing enough insight to help children challenge their parents' derisive attitudes and lobby realistically for changing what they feel is ureasonable or unfair. LeShan describes and strongly condemns adult behaviors involving physical abuse and violence and motivates children to secure help from a counselor or trusted adult should they feel they are in danger. She also discusses verbal abuse and its negative impact on self-esteem. Self-esteem, in fact, is of vital concern to LeShan throughout her book, which encourages young people to respect themselves and acknowledge their own opinions and needs.

Rue, Nancy N. *Coping with an Illiterate Parent.* 1990. New York: Rosen (0–8239–1070–9). Ages 12–16.

Can young people convince their illiterate parents to learn to read? Rue believes that while doing it won't be easy, it's both possible and important. An astute opening scenario, in which a child accidentally discovers his dad can't read, makes the problems that spring from illiteracy heartbreak-

ingly clear. Rue then speaks directly to teenage readers, discussing some reasons illiteracy still exists today and looking at how a parent's inability to read alters a young person's role in the family and changes family relationships. She encourages young people to confront their parents about the problem. Throughout the book runs a strong message about the importance of teens' own educations. A list of words crucial to personal health and safety is appended to the text.

Ryan, Elizabeth. *Straight Talk about Parents.* 1989. New York: Facts On File (0–8160–1526–0). Ages 14–18.

"My parents are too rigid"; "They don't give me enough privacy"; "They don't really listen to what I say." Complaints such as these are a normal part of adolescence, but teenagers don't have to let these problems get them down. There's a lot that can be done to make life less frustrating— even if parents aren't willing to cooperate. Communication is the key. That's the message of Ryan's book, which imparts sensible guidelines for smoothing out relationships at home. After explaining the difference between being assertive and being aggressive, Ryan reveals a few tricks of effective communication, including how to handle the embarrassing things parents always seem to say and do and how to determine if a disagreement with mom or dad is really "a battle worth waging." She also considers situations in which there are special family circumstances, such as divorce or family violence, supplying not only some well-reasoned advice but also a list of helpful organizations and hotlines to contact. Unfortunately, the book's unattractive dust jacket and its densely packed type deter a lot of potential readers who would surely have found some useful behavioral guideposts inside.

St. Pierre, Stephanie. *Everything You Need to Know When a Parent Is Out of Work.* 1991. New York: Rosen (0–8239–1217–6). Ages 12–15.

Don't be misled by this title. St. Pierre certainly doesn't cover "everything" in her sixty-four-page book, which is part of a series directed to teenagers who don't like to read (often called reluctant readers) and to young people who actually don't read very well. St. Pierre does, however, summarize a number of important factors related to joblessness, particularly as it affects the middle-class family. In an effort to remove some of the stigma associated with unemployment, she opens with a look at the various ways a parent can become jobless—illness, company layoffs, and so forth. She then clearly outlines the effects unemployment can have on a parent's behavior, family routines, and relationships. St. Pierre is least successful in treating the subject of financial assistance. Her discussion is too general to be of much practical use, and she conveys little sense of the bureaucratic tangle that must be endured. Despite that, her book is one of the few young adult nonfiction titles to treat the subject from the intimate perspective of the family unit rather than as a pervasive socioeconomic concern.

"When I'm home I'm still my parents' kid. When I'm out in the world, I'm a person."

—from *Changing Bodies, Changing Lives*

Taylor, Paul M., and Diane B. Taylor. *Coping with a Dysfunctional Family.* 1990. New York: Rosen (0–8239–1180–2). Ages 14–18.

Individuals who've heard the term *dysfunctional family* but don't really understand it will get a better idea of what it means through the words of five young adults whose families are destructive instead of nurturing. Varying in length and impact, the stories they tell expose family situations in which emotional neglect or drug, alcohol, or sexual abuse have compromised a teenager's self-esteem and distorted family roles and relationships. The text revolves around feelings, not facts. Its affecting personal narratives are intended to help teenagers see their

own situations more clearly, recognize the choices that are still open to them, and establish a frame of reference for facing their problems. The book demonstrates that breaking away from a dysfunctional family *is* possible, though certainly not easy.

Webb, Margot. *Coping with Overprotective Parents.* 1990. New York: Rosen (0–8239–1088–1). Ages 12–16.

Using examples of parent-child interactions many teens will recognize, Webb explains how and why parents may consciously or unconsciously repress their kids. She looks closely at the detrimental effects of using manipulative strategies to influence and discipline children and describes several techniques parents use, among them negative criticism, overindulgence, and false praise. Webb makes it plain to her teenage readers that she dislikes these particular methods of exerting control, but she never suggests that parents have no right to discipline or that the limits they set are unimportant. Questions scattered through the text will prompt classroom discussion, but the book will also rouse independent readers, whose overprotective parents may be making them feel more like "angry prisoners" than individuals ready to face adulthood.

Adoption, Blended Families, Divorce

Cohen, Shari. *Coping with Being Adopted.* 1988. New York: Rosen (0–8239–0770–8). Ages 12–16.

While teenagers wanting specifics for locating birth parents will find only a general overview here, Cohen is definitely sympathetic to their desire to fill in "the missing pieces" of their lives and ground their self-image in childhood experience. She's realistic about what such a search may mean to the adoptive family, though, and drawing on interviews she conducted with several adults, devotes some attention to clarifying the feelings of adoptive parents. Her hope is that lines of communication between adoptive parents and their children remain open even if a child does decide to search out a birth family. Cohen devotes most of her book to adoptees themselves, explaining the fantasies they create to establish their heritage and assessing the conflicting feelings—from gratitude and love to fear and resentment—they may have about their situation. She goes on to suggest ways adopted teens can handle cruel remarks from classmates or adoptive siblings, favoritism at home, and parental expectations. Cohen also offers sensitive insights into ways even common growing-up concerns can become particularly complicated for a child who's been adopted.

Getzoff, Ann, and Carolyn McClenahan. *Stepkids: A Survival Guide for Teenagers in Stepfamilies.* 1984. New York: Walker (0–8027–0757–2). Ages 12–16.

There are a number of teenage books about divorce, but comparatively few about the growing pains that come with a parent's remarriage. Written by two therapists, both of whom are members of "second" families, this book brings to light the problems teenagers in blended families often face and explains how assertive communication skills can help solve them. The authors look first at how someone's family history, adolescent development, and personal expectations about love influence the ability to deal with a stepparent. Specific challenges stepkids face—adjusting to a parent's homosexual relationship as well as more common problems, such as getting along with stepsiblings and conforming to new household rules—are then discussed, with the authors encouraging teenagers to seek help from a trained counselor if family difficulties become overwhelming. That bonding between families takes time and work is emphasized throughout the book, but Getzoff and McClenahan also make clear the rewards of patience and effort—a calmer, more stable situation at home, more realistic expectations about marriage, and a greater tolerance for individual differences.

Krementz, Jill. *How It Feels to Be Adopted.* 1982. New York: Knopf (0–394–53851–4); paper (0–394–75853–6). Ages 10–15.

They range in age from 8 to 16. They are black; they are white; they are Korean or Puerto Rican. Some of their families are homogeneous; others are mixed. One child lives in a single-parent family; his father is a Catholic priest. What the nineteen young people who speak out have in common is that they are adopted and, despite a few problems, they are happy in their adoptive homes. They also share a common curiosity about their roots, though not all want to seek out their birth parents. As one of the boys explains: "I hate to blame them, but it truly is their fault, and they don't have the right to reexamine their decision later on." Other kids disagree. Several, in fact, talk about the birth mothers they have located and are getting to know. Krementz's excellent black-and-white photographs give life to the individuals behind the words, and her smooth editing allows each speaker to remain distinctive. It's a book filled with eye-opening perspectives.

Krementz, Jill. *How It Feels When Parents Divorce.* 1984. New York: Knopf (0–394–54079–4); paper (0–394–75855–2). Ages 10–15.

Prolific author-photographer Krementz focuses her camera lens this time on nineteen children, who, like herself, have divorced parents. As in her book on adoption, she calls on young people representing a variety of ethnic, economic, and family situations to voice their feelings about a pivotal family issue. Ranging in age from 8 to 16, the children she spoke with also talk openly about their families and themselves in a series of nicely polished personal accounts. They express themselves with compelling candor, whether they are describing the shock of their parents' break-up, ensuing custody battles, or shuttling back and forth between households. Their unstudied testimonies validate the trauma of family dissolution and reveal the kind of personal strength needed to adapt to new circumstances. Like Krementz's *How It Feels to Be Adopted* and others in the author's How It Feels series, this is an insightful documentary, comforting in many ways. Young people can read it on their own or share it with their families.

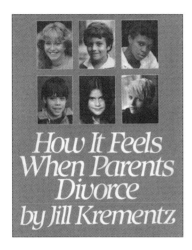

McGuire, Paula. *Putting It Together: Teenagers Talk about Family Breakups.* 1987. New York: Delacorte (0–385–29564–2). Ages 12–18.

Going one step further than Krementz does in *How It Feels When Parents Divorce,* McGuire provides perspectives from social workers and counselors who work with young people and their families. Even so, it's still the ingenuous responses of the teenagers she interviewed that give her book its power. The troubled pasts and unsettled presents of eighteen young people, who come from homes disrupted by a parent's death, a divorce, or abandonment, come across clearly in a series of uninterrupted personal narratives. The kids' honest, sometimes awkward, revelations present a compelling picture of divorce and of how young people survive its painful legacy.

"I've always known I was adopted, and when I was real little, I would go up to every pregnant lady I saw and ask her if she was planning to keep her baby or to give it up for adoption. They would all just stop dead in their tracks and look at me as though I were crazy!" Philip, age 15
—from *How It Feels to Be Adopted*

Rosenberg, Maxine B. *Growing Up Adopted.* 1989. New York: Bradbury (0–02–777912–2). Ages 10–14.

An adoptive mother, Rosenberg interviewed dozens of adults and children to find out how they felt about being adopted. Fourteen of them share their stories and feelings in this book. Though not necessarily content with the particulars, they all seem generally satisfied with their present situations. As was the case with the kids Krementz spoke with in *How It Feels to Be Adopted,* there was less accord in attitudes about birth parents. Rosenberg's adult respondents, many of whom discovered their adoptions by accident, were more resentful than the young people she spoke with, most of whom were told their backgrounds and were comfortable with the knowledge. It's the inclusion of adult perspectives of this kind that make Rosenberg's consideration of adoption distinctive.

Rosenberg, Maxine. *Talking about Stepfamilies.* 1990. New York: Bradbury (0–02–777913–0). Ages 10–14.

As in *Growing Up Adopted,* Rosenberg broadened her perspective by including the responses of adults as well as children in her collection of personal accounts. Here, her sixteen interviewees range in age from 8 to 41. With Rosenberg filling in the background, they lend insight into stepfamily dynamics and the changes that come along with such things as moving to a different house and altering routines and responsibilities. Rosenberg has been careful not to sugarcoat the testimonies, which express fear and hostility as well as the satisfaction of working to develop new friendships and strengthen family ties. The book is a frank, well-balanced view of a family phenomenon becoming commonplace. In a brief afterword, Rosenberg offers some practical guidelines for refining family accord, and she rounds out the text with two bibliographies, one for adults and one for children.

Being Homeless

Artenstein, Jeffrey. *Runaways: In Their Own Words: Kids Talking about Living on the Streets.* 1990. New York: St. Martins (0–312–93132–8). Ages 14–18.

Interviews with ten runaways staying at a Los Angeles halfway house while trying to get back on their feet offer a poignant, also shocking view of life on the streets for "between 730,000 and 1.3 million youth . . . who live, most of the time, by their own wits." Artenstein provides descriptive commentary through the book, which reverberates with the tough street jargon of the teenage addict, the prostitute, and the gang member. The kids, ranging in age from 10 to 17, have much history in common. Many come from broken homes; often they were abused by parents or involved with drugs. They are candid about their feelings ("being a whore like that is still better than being a normal person who

---

"I haven't had an address in years. I live in Riverside Park most of the time and go into the tunnels beneath the park when the weather's bad. There are old Amtrak tunnels in different parts of town that are underground cities. They have their own mayors and everything. In the salt mines near the piers, the boss is called the president." Dave Frank, age 22

—from *The Place I Call Home*

"... STRONG AND MOVING ." —JONATHAN KOZOL

THE PLACE I CALL HOME

FACES AND VOICES

OF HOMELESS TEENS

LOIS STAVSKY & I. E. MOZESON
PHOTOGRAPHS BY ROBERT HIRSCHFIELD

doesn't have anywhere to go") and about what they've had to face. Artenstein's epilogue, which briefly describes what happened to each of the teenagers he included in the text, serves as a frightening reminder of how difficult it is to turn the hope for a family and a better life into reality. This is a cautionary book with a grim message.

Stavsky, Lois, and I. E. Mozeson. *The Place I Call Home: Faces and Voices of Homeless Teens.* 1990. New York: Shapolsky (0–944007–81–3). Ages 14–18.

Teenagers participating in Stavsky's Manhattan dropout-prevention program interviewed peers who live on the streets for this disturbing collective profile. Language has been edited to "keep the book appropriate for younger readers and school libraries," but the brief first-person accounts still vividly convey the violence, poverty, and disaffection so much a part of some urban teens' lives. The young people, ranging in age from 14 to 22, speak matter-of-factly. A few express hope, but, like Tammy, a teen prostitute with AIDS, many sound discouraged and cynical; others seem unbelievably naive considering the experiences they describe. There are so many stories here (thirty-one in all) that eventually they begin to blur. But the book still sends a message that compels attention: stay off the streets—any way you can. Teenagers already faced with going it alone may find help through one of the organizations listed in the appendix.

Jill Krementz: Listening to Children

When she traded her sewing machine for a camera, Jill Krementz took her first step toward a career as a photojournalist. Hired by the *New York Herald Tribune* as its first woman photographer and later employed as correspondent for *Time,* she has since become a respected author of more than two dozen children's books that showcase her abilities as photographer and writer, among them *A Very Young Gardener* and *Lily Goes to the Playground.* She is also the author of the How It Feels series, an exceptional group of books about children and teenagers dealing with personal crises such as divorce, chronic illness, and adoption. The newest  in the series is *How It Feels to Live with a Physical Disability.* In "Listening to Children," which originally appeared in slightly longer form in *Worlds of Childhood: The Art and Craft of Writing for Children,* edited by William Zinsser (Houghton Mifflin, 1990), she explains how books for the How It Feels series are "born." At the same time, she reveals her fondness and respect for children and her devotion to her work.

When I think back to when I was ten, it was such a different life from what a ten-year-old lives today. There was no television, so what I knew about the outside world came mostly from books like the Nancy Drew series and *The Secret Garden.* I wasn't reading books like the ones I now write: I don't think there *were* any books like that. What girls of my generation were reading, in other words, was fiction and fantasy, and I'm sure all the work I've done, as a photographer and as a writer, has been a rebellion against that. I've been determined that children reading books today won't grow up as deprived of reality as I was.

I'd like to tell you how some of my books got born, especially the How It Feels books. I want to explain the process of how I choose and interview many different kinds of children and why I think their stories are helpful to other children and their families.

I started working and having heroes almost simultaneously—when I was nineteen. My heroes (and they still continue to influence me) were Jacob Riis, Lewis Hines, Dorothea Lange, and Gordon Parks—men and women who truly photographed *people* and did it with their heart. They used their pictures not only to gather information but to put it to constructive use. I've never been someone who would want to take pretty pictures and hang them on the wall and that's the end of it. I've always wanted to channel what I gather—to reprocess information in a way that's helpful to others.

Another one of my early heroes was Margaret Mead. When I was a young reporter for *Time* magazine I took Dr. Mead's anthropology course at Columbia, and I made a point of getting to know her. I think I realized very early that I wanted to do books about how people live. The course was basic anthropology, and that's what I've been doing ever since. What I like about anthropology is that it's nonjudgmental. In my How It Feels books, which deal with issues of loss that are highly complex—adoption, death, divorce, serious illness—I try to present every side of the issue without taking any side myself. What I learned from Margaret Mead was to be relentless and persistent in what I was going after, to work very hard, and to be a good listener. That course was the jumping-off point for my career as a writer of children's books.

My method is the same with every book. I take along two cameras (a Leica M-6 and a Nikon), a tape recorder, and a small spiral notebook. The notebook is for my field notes. It's never enough to just take pictures and to tape-record what a child says; I also need to know what the child was doing and observing and thinking and feeling, and what the people around him or her were thinking and saying. Then I convert all that information into a first-person narrative.

During this process I think of myself as the reader and try to make sure I understand the situation. I assume that if *I* understand it, any six-year-old will.

All the children in my books have the final right of approval. I feel very strongly about that. Some people are surprised—they think it's unprofessional. But I feel the same way about my books that I feel about my photography; that it's a collaboration between me and the person I'm working with. If I photograph someone, I want to use photographs that will please him.

After I go over the copy with the child and we've got what we think is good, we let his parents see it. I do this because it would be too easy to exploit children; they're extremely honest. The reason you get them to say such wonderful things is that they don't edit themselves if they trust you, and you can't violate that trust. Also, it's one thing to *talk* about your parents, but when children see what they've said in black and white and realize that it's going to be in a book, they may want to soften their remarks a little. I don't want these kids to hurt anybody. Also, I have to get the mother and father to sign off; that's a legal requirement because I'm dealing with minors. Fortunately, no parent has ever refused to sign; it's usually a question of some factual detail. They call us and say, "We have a few changes," and my heart is in my stomach. Then they say I've got it wrong about how old their dog is.

I think the reason parents are willing to stand by the material—even though it's often threatening to them—is that they respect what I'm trying to do.

Let me explain how I happened to get started doing these books. A friend of mine, Audrey Maas, died suddenly and unexpectedly after a short illness. She and her husband, Peter, and their little boy, John Michael, who was only eight, lived near us in the country, and in the days after Audrey's funeral we would go over and visit the house. I noticed that Peter had friends who had gone through a similar experience. But John Michael seemed very isolated, with nobody to talk to. So I thought it might be nice to try to do a book for other kids who were going through this. It would help them know that some of the weird feelings they were having weren't inappropriate. For instance, I had heard that John Michael told someone that he didn't understand why, right after his mother died, this perpetual cocktail party was going on. He had no way of knowing that such gatherings are a kind of grieving ritual that almost all societies have.

Because I had done six books that focused on *one* child—*Sweet Pea* and five Very Young books—my first thought was to follow one young girl through the death of her mother, probably of cancer, so that I would be on hand when it happened. But then I had second thoughts. Would my book help a little boy whose father dies? I also wondered what religion I should use. If I had an Episcopalian funeral, would it be relevant for a Jewish child? And how about the burial—should it be in a cemetery, or would the parent be cremated? Should the child have siblings, or should he or she be an only child? And I hadn't even thought about suicide, which is a surprisingly frequent cause of death among relatively young people. I realized that I would have to think more broadly.

At about that time I was asked to give a talk about my Very Young books to a group of librarians in Westchester County, New York. I told them about my project and read them a few passages about the children I had begun to interview. I asked them if they knew of any children in their schools who had lost a parent and who might like to participate. Within a week I had heard from eight of those librarians, and they all had wonderful kids for me; librarians are really in touch with the kids in their schools. I also put a notice in my alumni magazine and called the Big Brother organization. In the case of two of the children, Nick Davis and Susan Radin, their mothers had been close friends of mine before they died. Pretty soon I had the eighteen boys and girls I ended up using.

I pick my children carefully. I look for an age range from six to sixteen; at seventeen you're moving into an adult book. In fact, I don't have that many who are sixteen or six—just one or two. I want to be able to reach down to the six-year-olds, and if there's one six-year-old in the book, they feel that they have a friend they can latch onto. But after that I'm going for a median age. I want the book fairly evenly divided between girls and boys. I also want certain demographics—some blacks and Hispanics and Mexicans, not just little white children. I want both Christian and Jewish kids. I want some children who have brothers and sisters and some who don't. I want children who have been helped by psychiatrists and children who hate psychiatrists.

Most of all I want a range of issues. My books are designed to show both sides of every question. In *How It Feels When Parents Divorce,* for instance, there are various custody arrangements. I wanted to include a wide variety of possible structures. In *How It Feels to Be Adopted* I wanted it pretty evenly divided on the issue of "to search or not to search" for the birth parent, and also to cover children who had been searched *for.* My own opinion doesn't enter into it; nobody reading these books would know where I stand.

I tried for the same diversity in *How It Feels When a Parent Dies.* Of the Eighteen children, probably half want to go to the cemetery on Easter and Christmas, and the other half never want to go because it gives them the heebie-jeebies and just reminds them of their own mortality, or it makes them worry that something will happen to the surviving parent. But on one issue—whether or not the child should go to the parent's funeral—without exception the children who went to the funeral were glad and the ones who didn't go regretted it later. I feel very strongly about that issue, and I think it's one of the most important lessons that can be drawn from any of my books.

But there was one experience even worse for children than having a parent die. Divorce—as I found out when I was writing *How It Feels When Parents Divorce*—is the most painful of the traumas that my books deal with. Yet it's the most underestimated of all the injurious things that happen to children.

What makes divorce so long lasting in its effects has to do with self-image and ego. If a parent dies, he or she is all but deified by the surviving parent. It's always, "Oh, your father would have been so proud of you." It's a positive reinforcement of the missing parent, which, while it may sadden the child on one level, makes the child feel good about himself. Even in a "civilized" divorce, for example, it's not unusual to have one parent say to the child, "You'd better call your father and remind him to pick you up on Saturday." The implication is that the father doesn't care enough to remember.

With *How It Feels to Be Adopted,* I was surprised by how many parents turned me down. Many of them felt they had gone very far by even telling their children they were adopted. I always approach the parents first: I don't want to ask the children first and have them want to do it and then find their parents opposed, so that the parents become the bad guys. My ideal subject is therefore the child of a parent who, when I say I'm working on the project, says, "Well, I know Melissa loved *A Very Young Dancer*—in fact, it's grafted onto her chest, she's been carrying it around so much. It's fine with me, but why don't you call *her,* because the decision is totally hers." Then I feel that I'm home free, because first, that's the kind of parent who lets her child make decisions like that, and second, it's a parent who allows her child to have her own feelings.

I believe that all the children in my books have benefited from the experience. Often their teachers have told me how much better they're doing in school, or the children have written me themselves. They were so proud to be in the book, as well they might be; it makes *me* proud that they were included just for being articulate and in touch with their feelings and not because they made the baseball team or got all *A*'s.

Therefore one value of these books is that they enable children to listen to themselves. But their real value, I think, is that they enable children to listen to other children—to realize, often for the first time, that they are not alone in their situation.

Finally, I'd like to tell you about *How It Feels to Fight for Life,* which seemed like the natural fourth in the series. It's been by far the hardest and most painful one to write. I'm dealing with children who have a total of fourteen different illnesses and disabilities.

Actually, it's not the illness that I've focused on. I'm dealing primarily with the issue that the children are coping with—sibling rivalry, overprotective parents, financial stresses in the family, religious doubts, pain, hope, doctors who don't always listen to them, their relationships with schoolmates, and their struggle for independence at a time when illness makes them more dependent than ever on their parents.

As for the medical issues, that's why the book has taken me twice as long as the other How It Feels books. When I worked on the divorce book I at least knew what a divorce was; we all know that. But these illnesses are unfamiliar— you can't begin to interview a child until you've read the literature (and medical literature is a language unto itself). Before I could understand the problems that a child with lupus has, or a child with juvenile rheumatoid arthritis, I had to understand the disease, so that I would know what problems we were talking about.

I chose the title *How It Feels to Fight for Your Life* because it puts the child in an active, positive role. Even if the illness isn't literally life-threatening, what all these children are still fighting for is a normal life—one that is ennobled and that has a dignity they want and can reach for. My point is not to talk about a particular disease, or to tell people what it's like to be sick. I'm using children who I hope will be role models for other children. I'd like some other girl with rheumatoid arthritis to read about ten-year-old Lauren Dutton and say, "I don't really like playing the piano, but I like it enough so that if it's going to be good for my joints and make my fingers exercise, that's more interesting than the dumb exercises I'm doing with the therapist, and I might even learn to play the piano, too."

There's one young boy in my book, Spencer Gray, who had a kidney transplant. He's terrific. He can't do contact sports, and he's also quite small because all the steroids have stunted his growth, so he signed up with the ROTC program at school. I went to photograph him in his uniform, and this is what he told me: "Master Gunny Washington, who works with our group, told me right off to stop worrying about my size and not to think of myself as a novelty. What he said was, 'Size doesn't mean anything—it's the size of your heart that matters.' I go to training every day at seven-thirty, and on Tuesdays and Thursdays I have a drill at eight o'clock. We've won the city championship four years in a row. When I go to ROTC I forget that I'm smaller than the other kids, and a lot of the time I even forget that I'm sick. All I feel is real proud."

—Jill Krementz

FICTION

Doherty, Berlie. *Granny Was a Buffer Girl.* 1988. New York: Watts/Orchard (0–531–05754–2). Ages 14–18.

Preparing to leave England for a year abroad at school, Jess describes the extended family that has gathered to wish her well, weaving their stories into her own.

Duder, Tessa. *Jellybean.* 1986. New York: Viking (0–670–81235–8); paper (0–14–032114–4). Ages 11–14.

Geraldine (nicknamed Jellybean) lives with her single-parent mother, a cellist whose rigorous practice schedules leave Geraldine on her own, sitting in rehearsal halls or auditoriums for hours on end.

Fine, Anne. *My War with Goggle-Eyes.* 1989. Boston: Little, Brown (0–316–28314–2); Bantam, paper (0–553–28507–6). Ages 12–15.

Kitty Killin explains to a classmate distraught about her mother's boyfriend how stuffy Gerald Faulkner (Goggle-Eyes) came into Mrs. Killin's life and how Kitty tried to get him out.

Fox, Paula. *Monkey Island.* 1991. New York: Watts/Orchard/Richard Jackson (0–531–05962–6). Ages 10–14.

When his pregnant mother simply can't cope and disappears, 11-year-old Clay finds a home of sorts on the streets, where Buddy, a black teenager, and Calvin, a crabbed old alcoholic, manage to help him survive.

MacLachlan, Patricia. *Sarah, Plain and Tall.* 1985. New York: Harper/Charlotte Zolotow (0–06–024101–2); paper (0–06–440205–3). Ages 10–14.

Living on a prairie farm with their father, Anna and Caleb anxiously await the arrival of their possible stepmother, a woman who answered an advertisement their father placed in the newspaper for a mail-order bride.

Myers, Walter Dean. *Somewhere in the Darkness.* 1992. New York: Scholastic (0–590–42411–4). Ages 12–17.

Having escaped from the prison hospital, Crab shows up at the New York tenement where his son Jimmy lives, hoping the boy will forgive and learn to love him.

Newton, Suzanne. *I Will Call It Georgie's Blues*. 1983. New York: Dell, paper (0–440–94090–7). Ages 14–16.

The church congregation has no idea that their minister expects perfection from his family and metes out harsh punishment if he is disappointed. Fifteen-year-old Neal can cope with his father's demands. His little brother Georgie can't.

Okimoto, Jean Davies. *Molly by Any Other Name*. 1990. New York: Scholastic (0–590–42993–0). Ages 14–18.

Molly is Asian; her adoptive parents are white. After she discovers she can request a search for her birth mother when she reaches the age of 18, she decides to pursue answers to some long-suppressed questions.

Peck, Richard. *Father Figure*. 1978. New York: Dell, paper (0–440–20069–5). Ages 14–18.

Following his mother's death, Jim Atwater plans to be a substitute father to his kid brother. Then the boys' real father, whom they haven't seen in years, comes back into their lives.

Peck, Richard. *Unfinished Portrait of Jessica*. 1991. New York: Delacorte (0–385–30500–1). Ages 13–16.

Jessica has always idolized her dad, and when he leaves the family for good, she takes her anger out on her mother. Not until she spends time with her father at Christmas in beautiful Acapulco is she able to see him in unclouded light.

Pfeffer, Susan Beth. *The Year Without Michael*. 1987. New York: Bantam (0–553–05430–9); paper (0–553–27373–6). Ages 12–15.

A family suffers the tragic loss of one of their own when 13-year-old Michael leaves the house and never returns.

Porte, Barbara Ann. *I Only Made up the Roses*. 1987. New York: Greenwillow (0–688–05216–9). Ages 14–18.

Seventeen-year-old Cydra, a keen observer of those around her, introduces herself and her nurturing interracial family in a patchwork of interconnected stories.

Radin, Ruth Yaffe. *All Joseph Wanted*. 1991. New York: Macmillan (0–02–776641–6). Ages 11–14.

Though the fact that his mother can't read embarrasses Joseph, he's always been willing to help her. Then she becomes lost on a bus because she cannot read the street signs, and both Joseph and his mom realize things must change.

Sachs, Marilyn. *Baby Sister*. 1986. New York: Dutton (0–525–44213–8); Avon, paper (0–380–70358–0). Ages 13–16.

With few friends and few interests, plain Penny certainly isn't like her older sister Cass—attractive, energetic and independent, and out to challenge the world.

Taylor, Mildred. *Roll of Thunder, Hear My Cry*. 1976. New York: Dial (0–8037–7473–7); Bantam, paper (0–553–25450–2). Ages 11–14.

Unlike most black families in their small Mississippi town during the Depression, the Logans own the land they farm. Young Cassie tells the story of their struggle to keep it and to keep their family strong and together.

School Daze

COMPLETION OF SCHOOL HAS TRADITIONALLY been considered one of the steps necessary to enter adulthood, but *The State of America's Children: 1991,* a publication issued by the Children's Defense Fund, reveals some alarming news about today's youth and their attitudes toward school. Among other things, it tells us that too many young people leave school without the basic skills they need to function productively in society, and "every year at least 446,000 youths give up and drop out." The reasons for such grim revelations range from school violence and economic necessity to lack of school control and simple boredom. The following books include those that explore some of the causes of student disaffection along with titles that can help individuals identify their educational priorities and make the most of their school years.

"Schools and schooling are increasingly irrelevant to the great enterprises of the planet. No one believes anymore that scientists are trained in science classes or politicians in civics classes or poets in English classes. The truth is that schools don't really teach anything except how to obey orders." John Taylor Gatto, New York State Teacher of the Year, 1991

—from *The Teenage Liberation Handbook*

NONFICTION

Cohen, Susan, and Daniel Cohen. *Teenage Competition: A Survival Guide.* 1987. New York: Evans (0–87131–487–8). Ages 13–18.

Regarding competition as an inescapable part of life that can be detrimental as well as beneficial, the Cohens explain how to make certain that what a person strives for is really worthwhile. Using an easygoing, up-beat tone that will appeal to a teenage audience, they examine what's good and what's bad about competition and look at how rivalry shows up in family life, in peer-group and school situations, in sports, and in boy-girl relationships. Examples used to illustrate the discussion range from authentic sounding to simplistic and patronizing ("Let's imagine an intelligent observer from some distant planet, one who knows just about as much about human behavior as you know about the behavior of herring gulls . . ."). Despite that, the authors' view of how easily such things as SAT scores and popularity polls become false barometers of success makes intriguing reading, and their guidelines for setting more meaningful personal goals are grounded in common sense.

Cummings, Rhoda, and Gary Fisher. *The School Survival Guide for Kids with LD.* 1991. Minneapolis: Free Spirit, paper (0–915793–32–6). Ages 10–14.

In this helpful companion to *The Survival Guide for Kids with LD* (following, see Fisher), the authors explain learning disabilities (LD) in a way young readers will easily understand, then discuss specific strategies that will make classroom learning experiences more successful. Cartoon drawings and the authors' encouraging tone make the suggestions seem more like fun than schoolwork, whether the subject at hand is math, language, or interpersonal relationships. The authors include advice on organizing time and work, memorization tricks, and guidelines for improving handwriting, as well as alternatives to try when reading is a problem. Sensitive to the difficulties LD children have with peers, the authors also deal with ways kids can cope with teasing and handle other types of conflicts in the classroom or at recess. Though their discussion of peer relationships is general at best, their advice is certainly good: think before you act.

Delisle, James R., and Judy Galbraith. *The Gifted Kids Survival Guide II: A Sequel to the Original Gifted Kids Survival Guide (for Ages 11–18).* 1987. Minneapolis: Free Spirit, paper (0–915793–09–1). Ages 11–18.

What does being "gifted" mean? How does it relate to academic skills? The authors deal with those questions and separate myth from fact in a book that explains why being "gifted" is sometimes considered more a curse than a blessing. Upbeat in tone and illustrated with clever sketches and cartoon drawings, the book brings the problems of talented students to light and describes how being smart affects school performance as well as personal relationships. Along the way, the authors discuss the IQ as a measure of intelligence, suggest ways to get more out of class, and take a look at the special problems faced by young women who are gifted. A final section personalizes the discussion with profiles of two individuals, one 19 and the other 25, who stand out among their peers.

Detz, Joan. *You Mean I Have to Stand up and Say Something?* 1986. New York: Atheneum (0–689–31221–0). Ages 10–14.

Those who wince at the thought of public speaking may find Detz's encouraging guide just what they need to help them feel more confident. The chatty, encouraging text covers everything from picking a topic and judging an audience to quieting the jitters. There are also guidelines for using humor appropriately and tips for enlivening a presentation with visual aids. Illustrations add a cheerful note, concrete examples buttress the advice, and Detz suggests a few good resources for quotes, jokes, facts, and statistics.

Fisher, Gary L., and Rhoda Woods
   Cummings. *The Survival
   Guide for Kids with LD.* 1990.
   Minneapolis: Free Spirit,
   paper (0–915793–18–0).
   Ages 10–14.

While the *School Survival Guide* (Cummings and Fisher) concentrates on skills learning disabled students can use in class, this text focuses largely on facts about LD, or "learning different," as Fisher and Cummings call it. Emphasizing that having a learning disability "does *not* mean you are retarded! It does *not* mean you are dumb!" the authors discuss several different types of learning disabilities and the rationale behind LD special education programs. They also lend insight into the particular stresses LD youngsters face and suggest ways to deal with pressure from parents, teachers, and peers who don't always understand the impact a learning disability has on everyday life. Cartoon drawings, an open format, and bold headlines provide browser appeal.

"Most of my friends have cheated on tests in school at one time or another. . . . Nobody wants to cheat. But if it's a choice of being honest or of getting a grade, most kids will try for the A. That may sound wrong, but we didn't make the rules, we're just trying to get by." Michael, a student
   —from *Teenagers Talk about School*

Gilbert, Sara. *You Can Speak Up in
   Class.* 1991. New York: Morrow
   (0–688–09867–3); paper
   (0–688–10304–9).
   Ages 10–14.

Stressing that participating in class can reduce boredom and improve relationships with classmates as well as affect an individual's grades, Gilbert tenders some suggestions on overcoming speakers' reluctance. Using a selection of twenty "what if" scenarios ("What if you think you're stupid?" "What if you think you'll make the teacher mad?"), she identifies some of the common fears that cause students to be silent. Pairing the scenarios to "try this" responses, Gilbert summarizes each concern and offers concrete suggestions for communicating with more assurance. Though the information she presents is barely enough to make a book (cartoon drawings help extend the text to 54 generously spaced pages), Gilbert delivers it in a cheerful, well-organized manner and infuses it with plenty of encouragement.

Klein, David, and Marymae E. Klein.
   How Do You Know It's True?
   1984. New York: Scribner
   (0–684–18225–4).
   Ages 12–18.

Designed to help teenagers develop their powers of reasoning and hone their critical skills, this thought-provoking text both challenges and informs. Drawing concrete examples from home and school situations young people will recognize, the Kleins illustrate the often frustrating problem of distinguishing between truth, partial truth, and falsity. Particularly effective are discussions of the limitations of statistics and the effect personal prejudices have on interpretation. The Kleins occasionally resort to a few unsubstantiated assertions of their own, but the book is generally a useful, thought-provoking consideration of a subject about which little else exists specifically for teens.

Landau, Elaine. *Teenagers Talk about
   School . . . and Open Their
   Hearts about Their Concerns.*
   1989. Englewood Cliffs, N.J.:
   Messner (0–671–64568–4);
   paper (0–671–68148–6).
   Ages 12–18.

Personal testimonies based on interviews with a cross-section of American teens are the core of a book that presents a grim, even alarming view of American high schools today. Twenty-three junior high and high school students reflect on the educational and social aspects of the school environment they've experienced. Some express a love for learning and school, but most view school as a boring place, a place where academic, parental, and peer pressures collide to cause them pain and even humiliation. Unfortunately, Landau has not managed to preserve much of the personal voice of her speakers. There's a sameness about sentence structure and word usage that suggests a heavy editorial hand. It's the individualizing details in the accounts that leave an impact. Through them comes a sense of what kids really experience, whether it's the struggle of an inner-city boy whose school is run by gangs or the appeals of an Asian immigrant who's desperately trying to find friends.

Levine, Mel. *Keeping a Head in School: A Student's Book about Learning Abilities and Learning Disorders.* 1990. Cambridge, Mass.: Educators Publishing Service, paper (0–8388–2069–7). Ages 12–18.

A textbookish layout and 300-plus pages will scare off some teenage readers, but those who persevere will find a wealth of information on a topic frequently misunderstood. Levine explains a variety of difficulties and describes how they affect an individual in school and in social situations. He goes on to consider four basic operations—reading, writing, arithmetic, and spelling—identifying the particular problems students may face in each of these areas and suggesting simple strategies they can use when they are unable to process information in the usual way. Levine is realistic about the obstacles students with LD must overcome, but he urges them not to use their problem as an excuse to give up. He encourages them to look toward the future, assuring them that what they'll face in the post-school adult world will seem much less formidable than what they're dealing with now.

"'We are always getting ready to live but never living,' wrote Emerson. Don't let the schoolpeople write that on your tombstone."
        —from *The Teenage Liberation Handbook*

Like Fisher and Cumming's books about LD, cited earlier, which are written for a younger audience, this is a sensitive consideration.

Llewellyn, Grace. *The Teenage Liberation Handbook: How to Quit School and Get a Real Life and Education.* 1991. Eugene, Ore.: Lowry House, paper (0–9629591–0–3). Ages 14–18.

Lots of parents and teachers won't like this book. They'll argue that leaving school dooms a young person to a low-paying job and that Llewellyn's "experiential" approach to education is too unbalanced and too narrow. Having been a teacher, Llewellyn is familiar with the arguments. She counters them with some thought-provoking discussion that points to "unschooling," or "homeschooling," as a healthier, more reasonable choice than public or private school for most young people. Her contention is that "healthy kids can teach themselves what they need to know through books, various people, thinking, and other means." Reinforcing her text with enthusiastic commentary from self-taught teens, she explains how teenagers can overcome parental, legal, and practical roadblocks to home study and suggests creative activities and readings (she supplies a limited but excellent selection) to help teens handle subjects such as math, English, and social studies. Less dubious about the value of higher education than about compulsory schooling, the author encourages teenagers to prepare for college, tackling the problem of college entrance for those without high school credentials in a separate chapter that draws on advice gleaned from a sampling of responses from college admissions officers. Llewellyn's strident, recurring anti-school sentiments eventually become tiresome. But her enthusiasm for learning, her great faith in kids, and the wonderful educational possibilities she presents will make her book tantalizing reading for teens who can't make it in school but have the discipline and the passion to learn on their own.

Price, Janet R., and others. *The Rights of Students: The Basic ACLU Guide to a Student's Rights.* 1988. Carbondale, Ill.: Southern Illinois Univ., paper (0–8093–1423–1). Ages 12–18.

How can students know if their school rules are fair? When do students have the right to a hearing? These are but two of the many matters addressed in an accessible question-answer resource that gives high school students the facts about their public school rights. Discussions of the First Amendment and free education come first. Successive sections consider such topics as discipline, due process, personal appearance, disabilities, racial discrimination, and testing. Every chapter includes references to relevant court rulings and official school board and state decisions. An addendum describes the implications of the 1988 Hazelwood case, which concerned the censorship of school newspapers. This is a valuable resource teens should know about, even if it probably won't be a book they'll want to take home.

Ryan, Margaret. *So You Have to Give a Speech!* 1987. New York: Watts (0–531–10337–4). Ages 12–16.

Teenagers who find oral presentations difficult will appreciate this comforting speaker's manual that advocates thorough research and repeated practice to achieve success. A corporate speech writer, Ryan draws many of her colorful examples from her own speaker's portfolio and fills her very practical text with well-tested tips on everything from topic selection to final speech delivery. She also includes information about using the library and audiovisual aids and a bibliography of further readings about writing and speaking.

Salzman, Marian, and Teresa Reisgies. *Greetings from High School.* 1991. New York: Peterson's Guides, paper (1–56079–055–5). Ages 12–18.

This lively paperback catchall relies on questions, student comments, boxed lists, and quick-reference tips to inform its readers. Chapters on subjects such as romance, schoolwork, and stress outline issues on the minds of most teens. The book also introduces some unusual topics: for example, the pros and cons of different kinds of high schools (public, private, single-sex). Though the book does address some matters of interest to young people entering the work force right after high school, the text is really targeted to middle-class college-bound students. Not all subjects receive equal attention. Health-related matters fare the worst: safe sex gets two paragraphs; steroids, a big concern in school sports today, aren't even mentioned. But teenagers will grab the book anyway. They'll like its attractive cover, and the fact that the text is broken up into small chunks will be a great inducement to browsers.

Savage, John F. *Dyslexia: Understanding Reading Problems.* 1985. Englewood Cliffs, N.J.: Messner (0–671–542–89–3). Ages 11–13.

What is dyslexia? What causes it? Experts are divided, but Savage cuts through the forest of conflicting opinion to reveal a few things about which most authorities agree: dyslexia is a condition that causes problems in reading and writing; it is not the result of poor vision or hearing; sufferers are not intellectually impaired. In fact, most dyslexics have average or above-average intelligence. They must, however, learn differently. Savage explains what that means by taking a look at several methods used to teach dyslexic children. He also considers the condition's effect on an individual's self-esteem and explores the kinds of pressures dyslexics often face at school. Though less concerned with feelings and coping skills than facts, Savage's book is still a heartening overview that roundly debunks the idea that dyslexics are fated to fail.

Tchudi, Stephen. *The Young Learner's Handbook.* 1987. New York: Scribner (0–684–18676–4). Ages 11–14.

Tchudi speaks to young people with an unusual problem. They *love knowledge,* and they are excited enough about learning to want to investigate a subject outside the classroom. Tchudi helps them get started, beginning with tips on how to create a comfortable workplace. A discussion of specific learning skills follows, with Tchudi advising on everything from framing questions and gathering material from the library to systematizing findings so they can be referred to again and again. Tchudi's enthusiastic tone reflects his own delight in independent learning.

Wirths, Claudine G., and Mary Bowman-Kruhm. *I Hate School: How to Hang in & When to Drop Out.* 1986. New York: Harper (0–690–04556–5); paper (0–06–446054–1). Ages 13–17.

A wealth of material exists for the young adult preparing for college or planning a career, but little is available for a teenager simply trying to get through a tough school day. Wirths and Bowman-Kruhm offer one of the few such support books. Friendly and sympathetic in tone, it speaks to restless, unmotivated students, encouraging them to stay in school—if only to avoid a lifetime of dead-end, low-paying work. The authors look briefly at the impact of school social life on student performance and attitude, but their real concern is study skills. Cartoon characters expressing common gripes ("Trying to do homework in my house is impossible," or "Are there any shortcuts to reading?") inaugurate discussion of particular topics that the authors then explore in uncritical, reassuring terms. It's a serious attempt to help kids make the most of their classroom experience, with clever art that will attract kids who like to browse the shelves.

FICTION

Carter, Alden R. *Wart, Son of Toad.* 1985. New York: Putnam (0–448–47770–X). Ages 14–18.

Steve Michaels knows he'd be happier studying auto mechanics than going off to college, but he can't convince his stubborn, academically oriented father to let him try.

Cormier, Robert. *The Chocolate War.* 1974. New York: Pantheon (0–394–82805–4); Dell, paper (0–440–94459–7). Ages 14–18.

When Jerry Renault refuses to sell candy for his parochial school, he makes a powerful enemy of Brother Leon, his instructor, who runs things by turning a blind eye on the activities of a vicious school gang. A sequel, *Beyond the Chocolate War,* set in the same school milieu, was published in 1985.

Davis, Jenny. *Sex Education.* 1988. New York: Watts/Orchard/Richard Jackson (0–531–05756–9); Dell, paper (0–440–20483–6). Ages 14–18.

Abandoning the curriculum to teach a unit on sex education, a ninth-grade biology teacher begins with an unusual project: find someone to care about. Sixteen-year-old Livvie and classmate David Kindler choose fragile, pregnant Maggie Parker, Livvie's new neighbor, as the focus of their concern.

Hermes, Patricia. *I Hate Being Gifted.* 1990. New York: Putnam (0–399–21687–1). Ages 11–14.

Adults tell KT it's an honor to be in LEAP, the Learning Enrichment Activity Program for gifted students. But KT knows better. She's seen her "weirdo" teacher and heard "LEAP creep" taunts often enough to make her certain her entire sixth-grade year will be a disaster.

Klass, Sheila Solomon. *The Bennington Stitch.* 1985. New York: Scribner (0–684–18436–2); Bantam, paper (0–553–26049–9). Ages 14–18.

Amy Hamilton is a skilled seamstress and cook, and she loves to do both. But her mother wants her to abandon her favorite activities and attend tony Bennington College where she'll pursue a different kind of program.

Naylor, Phyllis. *The Year of the Gopher.* 1987. New York: Atheneum (0–689–31333–0); Bantam, paper (0–553–27131–8). Ages 14–18.

A Minneapolis high school senior sabotages his parents' plans to send him off to college for a law degree.

Peck, Richard. *Princess Ashley.* 1987. New York: Delacorte (0–385–29561–8); Dell, paper (0–440–20206–X). Ages 12–15.

Sophomore Chelsea Olinter feels wonderful when she's invited to join the most popular crowd in her new school—until she discovers she's been asked because her mother is a high school guidance counselor.

Stone, Bruce. *Been Clever Forever.* 1988. New York: Harper (0–06–447013–X). Ages 14–18.

Tenth grader Stephen A. Douglass is a smart wisecracker and everyone expects a lot from him. It takes a run-in with a disturbed teacher to help him understand that the only expectations he needs to live up to are his own.

Wolff, Virginia Euwer. *Probably Still Nick Swansen.* 1988. New York: Holt (0–8050–0701–6). Ages 14–18.

Nick Swansen has minimal brain dysfunction. Although he isn't certain exactly what that is, he knows that's why he's in Special Ed Room 19. But even though he needs some extra help with lessons, he sees no reason why he can't take his pretty former classmate to the school prom.

Me, Myself, and I

DEVELOPING A REALISTIC SENSE of self is one of the most difficult developmental tasks of adolescence. Most teenagers have a hard time accepting the fact that it's not possible to be perfect; few realize how their self-image affects their relationships with parents, friends, and the opposite sex. Identity is a common theme in realistic young adult fiction, but only recently have nonfiction writers begun to deal with it in a self-help context. Terms such as *positive self-talk, assertiveness,* and *codependency* and theories associated with them, familiar in adult books on self-affirmation, are trickling down into teenage materials. Self-concept workbooks are now being used in some schools, while books on everything from setting personal goals to getting on better with friends are now available to independent readers.

"I'm not sure what I'm aiming for when I look in the mirror.
Some days I'm happy with the way I look, others I'm not.
I don't know if this is to do with my lipstick or my attitude.
The sad part is that I've come to hate my body so much,
I blame it for everything." Helen, age 23
—from *How Do I Look?*

NONFICTION

Self-Esteem

Barry, Lynda. *Come Over, Come Over.* 1990. New York: HarperPerennial, paper (0–06–096504–5). Ages 15–18.

This book bears no resemblance to a young adult self-help manual. It's actually a collection of comics culled from the multi-talented Barry's syndicated strip, "Ernie Pook's Comeek." But it's much more than an entertaining miscellany of cartoons. Maybonne Mullen, a freckle-faced redhead who may well be Barry's alter ego, is the featured character. The strips chronicle her fourteenth year—from arguments with her mother and experiments with cigarettes, alcohol, and boys to a rapprochement with her estranged dad. Barry's quirky, sophisticated humor won't appeal to everyone, but the frank, poignant collection captures the frustrations, the hopes, and the pleasures of growing up female in a refreshing new way. Girls can identify with Maybonne and laugh at her at the same time.

Bode, Janet. *Beating the Odds: Stories of Unexpected Achievers.* 1991. New York: Watts (0–531–15230–8). Ages 12–18.

Eleven young adults who've overcome enormous odds tell how they feel about themselves and what they've accomplished in a collection of upbeat profiles that includes one cartoon story. Unfortunately the picture-story doesn't work very well. Sandwiched between personal narratives, it is likely to be ignored. And while it deals with a boy's experience in an abusive home, it is far less affecting than the detailed, unpretentious first-person narratives surrounding it. They are more dramatic and more poignant. Declaring that self-esteem is the "only drug" she needs, Keisha describes what it's like to live in a welfare hotel overrun with drug pushers; 18-year-old Pawnee, a teenage mother, talks about making her daughter proud of her; and Matthew, a college freshman who was imprisoned at the age of 16 for

shooting someone, explains how he refocused his life. Bode alternates kids' words with commentary from adults—some professional counselors and teachers,

some simply adults who've overcome difficult situations in their own lives. Their combined testimonies provide readers with a firm, but also realistic, sense of possibilities, which Bode reinforces with simple but important advice on how to begin to turn life around: "read, reach out, keep busy, keep trying."

Dawson, Jill. *How Do I Look?* 1991. London, England: Virago, paper (1–85381–222–6). Ages 15–18.

Though this book's British perspective will deter some American readers, its subject translates well into American experience. Setting the stage with the story of her own seven-year battle with eating disorders, Dawson presents a patchwork of excerpts from letters and interviews she conducted with an articulate multicultural selection of British women, ranging in age from 17 into their early 20s. Some angry and confused, some confident and happy, the young women reflect on a variety of contemporary feminist issues, among them, cultural ideals of female perfection, eating disorders as a misguided means of self-determination, and the use of clothing to make personal and political statements. Taken together, their testimonies reveal an intriguing slice of modern culture. Not a downbeat, strident book of behavioral guideposts, this is, instead, a sensitive, forthright consideration of important women's issues meant to provoke thought, not shape it.

"You need positive things in your life. You need to be able to say, 'I did that kid's workshop and, *damn* it went well.' You need things you can brag about inside yourself. . . . That's my drug, self-esteem." Keisha, age 16
—from *Beating the Odds*

Heine, Arthur J. *Surviving after High School: Overcoming Life's Hurdles*. 1991. Virginia Beach, Va.: J-Mart Press (0–9628376–0–1). Ages 16–up.

Directed to emancipated teens or high school graduates ready to live independently, Heine's book is filled with practical advice about entering the "jungle called 'real life.'" With a dash of homespun philosophy, his text spells out how to become self-sufficient, including advice on everything from job hunting to buying a car and renting an apartment. Using reproductions of actual forms, Heine explains important facts about insurance, taxes, leases, and loan agreements, then supplies a few words about managing health concerns—some counsel about safe sex, plus tips on exercise and nutrition. Chapters conclude with space for jotting down notes.

Johnson, Julie Tallard. *Celebrate You: Building Your Self Esteem*. 1991. Minneapolis: Lerner (0–8225–0046–9). Ages 12–15.

Johnson encourages teenagers to take pride in themselves in this upbeat 72-page guide that touches on both the practical and the spiritual. A quiz sets the stage for the simply written text that describes how negative thoughts and outside circumstances influence one's self-concept. Johnson explains the concept of "positive self-talk" and supplies a list of simple ways to boost the spirits: exercise, talk to a supportive friend, and meditate, among them. She also talks about making choices and accepting responsibility for them, an integral part of building self-esteem. Concise comments from teenagers appear throughout the text, and Johnson contributes personal perspective in a final chapter in which she speaks of her own childhood lack of confidence and of the strength she now derives from her belief in "a power greater than all the troubles and challenges you face." She doesn't proselytize, but her message is unmistakable. The author is a psychotherapist who works with teens.

Klein, David, and Marymae E. Klein. *Your Parents and Yourself: Alike/ Unlike/Agreeing/Disagreeing*. 1986. New York: Scribner (0–684–18684–5). Ages 14–17.

"My mother was a talented musician. . . . Do I have the same talent?" "Whom will I grow up to be like—my real father or my stepfather?" "My father is a successful doctor. Does this mean I should go to medical school?" Contending that few teenagers want to be *just like* mom or dad, the Kleins explore the subtle influences parents have on their kids. They view the effects of inherited as well as environmental factors on developing individuality, touching lightly on such topics as being smart, child-rearing practices, morals, and economic background. Their treatment becomes more focused in final chapters, where they advise teenagers on how to cope with parental expectations related to college or career. A thought-provoking book that reassures readers there's plenty of room to be different.

LeShan, Eda. *What Makes You So Special*. 1992. New York: Dial (0–8037–1155–7). Ages 10–14.

Despite your desire to be "like everyone else," you are special, you are different. That's the message of LeShan's latest book, which explores the environmental and hereditary forces that mold individuality. LeShan's flowing, nontechnical narrative is filled with concrete examples that illustrate how home life, school experiences, peers, family background, and world events influence self-concept and help forge identity. As she often does in her books, the author draws incidents from her own life (she was born in 1922) to furnish readers with historical perspective. Understanding but firm in her personal convictions, she functions here as a compassionate, perceptive advocate of self-awareness whose respect for individual differences and love of life echo through the text.

A Few Words with Eda LeShan

Though self-help books are a relatively recent publishing phenomenon, they aren't new to Eda LeShan. She's been writing them, along with books for adults, for more than twenty years. Her first children's book, *What Makes Me Feel This Way? Growing Up with Human Emotions,* was published in 1972. A parent educational consultant who's discussed the subject of parenting on both radio and television, she now writes a *Newsday* column for readers over 60. She hasn't forgotten children, though.

SZ: You wrote several books for adults before your wrote *What Makes Me Feel This Way?* Why did you decide to write a book for kids?

EL: I had written an article for *Parents* magazine on children's fears, and the children's book editor called me up and asked if I had ever thought about writing a book on emotions for children. I never had. I assumed I would always be writing books for adults, but it was an intriguing idea. I thought I'd try it, so I sat down in the country in the summertime and started working. I wrote the book in three weeks. The reason I was able to do that was that I was writing the book for myself as a child. All my children's books have arisen out of that feeling. They have been on things that I would have wanted somebody to tell me about or to say to me when I was growing up.

SZ: Do you enjoy writing children's books more than adult books?

EL: Oh yes. Much more than books for grownups.

SZ: Your latest book, *What Makes You So Special,* is quite different from your other books for children. You tackle a much broader topic.

EL: Oh, you saw the galleys, didn't you?

SZ: Yes. Your editor sent me a set. Why did you choose this topic?

EL: I suppose it just occurred to me that we really needed a book that covered the whole waterfront, all the different influences on children. I think encouraging kids to want to be themselves is one of the biggest problems we have today. Children face terrible pressure to be like everybody else. I thought this book might be a little counterpoint to some of that. It contains much more social background and information about the climate of life than my other children's books do.

SZ: You discuss identity from a very broad perspective. You talk about school influences, role models, heredity . . .

EL: You know, I wrote to everybody I know who is in the children's publishing business, and I went to several libraries. I told them all what the book was about and what the various chapter headings were going to be. And the only relevant books I could find were on heredity. I think this general business of how you develop self-esteem and self-acceptance has not been written about for kids.

SZ: Why do you integrate so many of your own experiences into your books?

EL: It's because I learned much more from psychotherapy than I ever learned in school. I became very introspective and went back into my own childhood. I know it sounds terribly egotistical, but I really feel I understand children better than most child psychologists. I use myself as an instrument, and I've faced a great many things in my life. After about thirty years on and off psychotherapy I have total recall to the age of two. I use all of that, and I think it's a lot more important than what you study in a laboratory. Children can identify with me because I share feelings with them. My books aren't pedantic or academic. They're very personal. I think that's what children want . . . role models and people who know how they're feeling because they've been through it themselves.

SZ: You are certainly one of the first authors to write what's now being called self-help literature.

EL: That's right. In a way it's kind of sad. So many other books have come out on death and divorce and all these other subjects. I introduced the subjects first, but many of my books are now remaindered or out of print.

SZ: Why do you think self-help books for children have proliferated?

EL: Publishers must have found them successful. There's much more awareness that children react very strongly to such traumas as death and divorce. And parents and educators now recognize that children need help with their feelings.

Levinson, Nancy, and Joanne Rocklin. *Getting High in Natural Ways: An Infobook for Young People of All Ages.* 1986. Claremont, Calif.: Hunter House, paper (0–89793–036–3). Ages 14–18.

A children's book author and a clinical psychologist take a look at the intricate relationship between feelings and physical response and explain how to exploit the connection to become happier and more confident. Steering clear of the saccharine enthusiasm so prevalent in this kind of self-help material, the writers suggest sensible ways to achieve a "natural high," among them: meditating, physical exercise, competitive activities, listening to music, and even crying. The fill-in-the-blank charts accompanying most chapters make the text especially appealing for a teenager's home bookshelf, but because it's one of the best of the few books about "getting high" without drugs, schools and libraries will find it valuable, too.

McFarland, Rhoda. *Coping through Assertiveness*. 1986. New York: Rosen (0–8239–0680–9). Ages 12–16.

Expressing emotions honestly and directly without threatening others is one of the most difficult developmental lessons teenagers must learn. McFarland, who has been both a teacher and counselor, talks earnestly about the problems involved. Vignettes about teenagers at school and at home provide the background for advice about dealing with parents, teachers, friends, relatives, and the opposite sex. The author makes clear the distinction between aggressive and assertive communication as she discusses how to handle a variety of situations, from expressing a verbal "no," a "right . . . you do not have to justify and defend," to preventing someone from cutting in the lunch line. At the same time she explains the passive-aggressive games people play and the anger that comes from having to hide real feelings when a person becomes involved in one of them.

Olney, Ross R., and Patricia J. Olney. *Imaging: Think Your Way to Success in Sports and Classroom Activities*. 1985. New York: Atheneum (0–689–31121–4). Ages 15–18.

"It is true that a person can do almost anything if they really want it and really set their mind to it." Too optimistic? The Olneys certainly don't think so, and they explain why. Then they describe how imagining positive experiences (visualization) can promote the self-confidence necessary to succeed in a wide variety of activities—from weight loss to improving concentration to kicking the smoking habit. To substantiate their claims, they review scientific findings that demonstrate links between positive thinking and physical and mental well-being. It's a premise that will certainly attract teenagers interested in self-improvement, and the authors handle the material in the approachable, upbeat manner of many adult popular psychology books. But they also occasionally oversimplify ("Positive thinking can effect positive cures"), which makes their otherwise intriguing book best suited to discerning high school readers who will investigate the topic further before they become true believers.

Porterfield, Kay Marie. *Coping with Codependency*. 1991. New York: Rosen (0–82339–1198–5). Ages 14–18.

Porterfield deals with a trendy topic, incorporating just enough of the jargon of adult "recovery" books to give her text an authentic tone. A teacher with a degree in counseling, she explains how families unable to function normally—because of a family crisis or a substance abuser in the home, for example—can create insecure "codependent" family members who deny their feelings and are unable to handle relationships in healthy ways. Without exploiting teen insecurities, she explains some of the behaviors and thought patterns characteristic of codependents and offers encouragement and practical, if sometimes simplistic, guidance to help young people try to retake control of their lives.

Smith, Lucinda Irwin. *Growing Up Female*. 1987. Englewood Cliffs, N.J.: Messner (0–671–63445–3). Ages 12–15.

Self-determination in this complicated world is the subject of a book that begins with a look at such bench marks in American women's history as suffrage and the rise of the feminist movement in the 1960s. Drawing together personal accounts from individuals who have chosen traditional and nontraditional women's roles, the author then presents an encouraging overview of the career choices open to young women today. Other matters—among them, relationships with family and with the opposite sex, fitness, pregnancy—are also discussed in terms of available options. Health issues that may influence decision making about sexual relationships are not well defined; information on sexually transmitted diseases, for example, will need to be obtained elsewhere. Still, Smith puts growing up female into a broader context than most girls' books about adolescence by demonstrating how the struggles of a young woman's forebears helped shape the alternatives she has today and may have in the future.

Yepsen, Roger. *Smarten Up!*
   1990. Boston: Little, Brown
   (0–316–96864–1). Ages 11–14.

"The keenest minds have sharpened themselves on simple things," writes the author in a wonderfully unusual look at brain power. How does the brain actually work? Yepsen summarizes the physiology, then goes on to describe what the organ needs to function most efficiently and how rest, exercise, and a nutritious diet each play a part. He also suggests techniques for improving memory and coping with the effects outside factors such as light, sound, and weather have on the ability to think clearly. Creativity has a chapter of its own, filled with exercises and brain teasers designed to stretch the imagination. Yepsen looks last at how meditation can help overcome anxiety and focus thought and how individuals can take advantage of the creative natural "high" researchers call "flow."

Social Sense

Bode, Janet. *Different Worlds:
   Interracial and Cross-Cultural
   Dating.* 1989. New York:
   Watts (0–531–10663–2).
   Ages 12–18.

Concentrating on five teenage couples, Bode investigates a complicated social issue, concluding that despite "the stars in your eyes," interracial or interethnic relationships are rarely easy to maintain. She draws heavily on interviews with parents, educators, and health professionals, as well as on encounters with young people themselves, as she explores the reactions of parents and friends to interdating and looks at the insidious nature of prejudice,

which, she writes, can turn "you and your partner into a trio." Experts lend insight into society's views on the subject, the reasons some teenagers are attracted to individuals of a different race or background, and how young adults can deal realistically with the pressures they'll almost surely face. Kathlyn Gay's *The Rainbow Effect* (see the index), which looks at interracial and interethnic families, is another useful resource that deals with related issues.

LeShan, Eda. *When Kids Drive Kids
   Crazy.* 1990. New York: Dial
   (0–8037–0866–1). Ages 10–14.

"I remember very well how I felt when I was growing up and someone made fun of me, or a friend deserted me, or I felt very unpopular," recalls LeShan, who acknowledges how tough it is to be a kid, especially in today's complicated world. Writing in the same honest, sympathetic voice she has used in other books for young people, she mixes personal childhood memories with anecdotes about ordinary kids to establish the rationale underlying many hurtful, bewildering behaviors. Her scope is broad; she considers not only peer influence and the impact of physical and emotional maturation, but also confusing messages about sex and sex-role stereotypes that bombard today's young. A chapter entitled "Special Problems" sensitively discusses kids coping with physical challenges or extraordinary outside pressures, such as poverty, prejudice, or community violence. The idea that our relationships help shape us comes through loud and clear.

"I really like my best friend a lot. So why am I so nasty to her sometimes? If a teacher yells at me or me and my mom have a fight before school, I start taking my bad mood out on my friend. I'm scared of losing her and don't know how to stop this." Jessica, student

—from *Changes and Choices*

McCoy, Kathy. *Changes and Choices: A Junior High Survival Guide.* 1989. New York: Putnam/Perigee, paper (0–399–51566–6). Ages 11–15.

The coauthor of the *Teenage Body Book* and a columnist for *Seventeen* magazine addresses 12- to 15-year-olds about some of the challenges they face as they become physically and emotionally mature. Managing to be both sensible and upbeat, McCoy talks first about dealing with the emotional ups and downs that come with adolescence. Complaints about parents (''They favor my brother''; ''They don't give me any privacy''; ''They expect too much'') fill a chapter on changing family relationships. Thorough discussions of friendships, school, and a variety of social situations follow, with McCoy explaining how to cope with such common concerns as first love, teacher trouble, and embarrassing physical changes. Tough topics—the use of recreational drugs and alcohol and premarital sex—are dealt with in a separate section. McCoy is firm but not shrill in her disapproval of all three activities for this age group. The book's attractive cover photograph should make browsers eager to pick up the oversized paperback.

Post, Elizabeth L., and Joan M. Coles. *Emily Post Talks with Teens about Manners and Etiquette.* 1986. New York: Harper (0–06–096117–1). Ages 12–16.

Etiquette consultant Coles and Post, the granddaughter of ''mistress of manners'' Emily Post, teamed up with the idea of making teenagers more ''comfortable'' with manners. Mixing tried-and-still-true directives with manners guidelines specifically for today's young people, the pair provides up-to-date perspectives on the social graces, covering everything from dating behavior and eating etiquette to conduct during a job interview. The book's peppy humor gets a bit cloying now and then, but the advice itself is a solid blend of good sense and consideration for others.

Ré, Judith, and Meg F. Schneider. *Social Savvy: A Teenager's Guide to Feeling Confident in Any Situation.* 1991. New York: Summit (0–671–69023–X). Ages 12–16.

Though this book won't prepare teens for every situation as its subtitle implies, it does contain lots of useful advice. Ré, who runs weekend courses in social behavior for young adults, supplies the agreeable voice of the text, which proceeds from the premise that good manners are a sign of respect and consideration for others,

not just a bunch of silly rules. Using quick-read scenarios depicting specific manners dilemmas (''Miserable Moments'') and their solutions, the authors discuss such familiar etiquette quandaries as making introductions and restaurant protocol, as well as a few not routinely covered in this kind of book—dealing with friction between one's friends or negotiating for a bigger allowance, for example. The most rigid guidelines appear in the section on table manners. Unfortunately, a few of these rules (e.g., the etiquette for removing paper from a straw) cross the silliness line the authors seemed so anxious to avoid.

FICTION

Busselle, Rebecca. *Bathing Ugly.*
1989. New York: Watts/
Orchard/Richard Jackson
(0–531–05801–8); Dell, paper
(0–0440–20921–8). Ages 11–14.

Smart, overweight Betsy quietly and deter-
minedly diets only to discover that losing
weight has little effect on her friendships—
her enemies don't suddenly mellow; girls
who've befriended her don't care whether
she's fat or thin.

Cole, Brock. *Celine.* 1989. New
York: Farrar (0–374–31234–6).
Ages 14–18.

Living with her stepmother in a Chicago
flat, high school junior Celine finds herself
drawn to her neighbor Jacob, a second
grader caught up in the pain of his parents'
separation. Through relating to each other,
they learn about themselves.

Cole, Brock. *The Goats.* 1987. New
York: Farrar (0–374–32678–9);
paper (0–374–42575–2).
Ages 12–15.

Stripped, then left on a remote island as
part of a cruel summer-camp joke, Laura
and Howie escape from the island and run
away, discovering much about themselves
and about each other as they struggle to
survive.

Deuker, Carl. *On the Devil's Court.*
1989. Boston: Little, Brown
(0–316–13147–1). Ages 14–18.

Lacking confidence in the face of his brilliant father's expectations and uneasy after
his family's move, Joe Faust seeks solace
on the basketball court.

Hall, Lynn. *Just One Friend.*
1985. New York: Scribner
(0–648–18471–0). Ages 14–18.

Following three years of special education,
Dory Kjellings is not looking forward to
being mainstreamed into regular high
school. She thinks she can do it, though,

if she can just get a friend to cross the
threshold with her on the first day of class.

Hall, Lynn. *The Solitary.* 1986.
New York: Macmillan
(0–684–18724–8); paper
(0–02–043315–8). Ages 14–18.

High school graduate Jane Cahill returns to
the backwoods cabin where she spent her
childhood, hoping to become self-reliant
and forget her tragic past.

Koertge, Ron. *Boy in the Moon.*
1990. Boston: Little, Brown
(0–316–50102–6). Ages 14–18.

A high school senior, Nick worries about
his acne, his physique, and his lack of
sexual experience, especially now that he's
becoming increasingly attracted to his longtime friend and classmate, Frieda.

Koertge, Ron. *Mariposa Blues.*
1991. Boston: Little, Brown
(0–316–50103–4). Ages 11–14.

Being told he looks just like his father, a
successful horse trainer, makes Graham
furious. That's the last thing he wants to
hear when he's trying so desperately to get
people to accept him for himself.

Lipsyte, Robert. *One Fat Summer.*
1977. New York: Harper-Collins
(0–06–023896–8); Bantam,
paper (0–553–25591–6).
Ages 12–15.

Being overweight and having a father who
demands a lot are difficult burdens for
Bobby Marks—until one telling summer
when he learns that being thin and tough
isn't nearly as important as being compassionate and doing the right thing.

Myers, Walter Dean. *Fallen Angels.*
1988. New York: Scholastic
(0–590–40942–5); paper
(0–590–40943–3). Ages 15–18.

More to postpose a dead-end life in Harlem
than because of political principles,
17-year-old Richie Perry enlists in the army.
The friendships he makes among fellow
soldiers in Vietnam change his life forever.

Myers, Walter Dean. *Scorpions.*
  1988. New York: Harper
  (0–06–024364–3); paper
  (0–06–447066–0). Ages 12–15.

Although his friend Tito tries to discourage
him from becoming involved in his neighborhood gang, 12-year-old Jamal covets the
promise of power enough to go to a gang
meeting. He brings along his good friend
Tito, and he also brings a gun.

Paulsen, Gary. *The Island.* 1988.
  New York: Watts/Orchard/Richard
  Jackson (0–531–05749–6); Dell,
  paper (0–440–20632–4).
  Ages 14–16.

Despite pleas from his parents, who want
him to come home, and visits from a nosey
reporter and an idiotic psychiatist, 15-year-
old Wil Neuton still manages to puzzle out
the essence of himself while he sits in self-
imposed exile on an island near his home.

Rodowsky, Colby. *Sydney, Herself.*
  1989. New York: Farrar
  (0–374–30649–4). Ages 12–15.

To blunt scary feelings about who she is
and help her face a problematic life with
her single-parent mom, Sydney Downie
weaves an elaborate fantasy: she imagines
herself to be the daughter of a famous Aus-
tralian rock musician.

Rostowski, Margaret I. *The Best
  of Friends.* 1989. New York:
  Harper (0–06–025104–2).
  Ages 14–18.

Three Utah teenagers—peace activist Sarah,
Sarah's brother Dan, and their close friend
Will—discover that their divergent political views of the Vietnam War are affecting
their friendship.

Slepian, Jan. *Risk 'n Roses.* 1990.
  New York: Putnam/Philomel
  (0–399–2219–7). Ages 12–14.

There's something about Jean Persico that
makes 11-year-old Skip, a lonely newcomer

to the neighborhood, want her for a friend.
But when Jean draws Skip's developmen-
tally disabled older sister into a cruel prank,
Skip finds herself caught between family
loyalty and her desperate desire to belong.

Staples, Suzanne Fisher. *Shabanu:
  Daughter of the Wind.* 1989. New
  York: Knopf (0–394–84815–2).
  Ages 13–15.

Pledged to be married to a much older man
whom she does not love, a Pakistani girl
is caught between her personal feelings and
her family's strict customs.

Wersba, Barbara. *Fat.* 1987. New
  York: Harper (0–06–026415–2);
  Dell, paper (0–440–20537–9).
  Ages 14–18.

Rita Formica loves Robert, a handsome
jock who comes with his family to stay in
her resort hometown. But Rita weighs two
hundred pounds, and the only person who
seems willing to overlook the fact is eccen-
tric Arnold, her kind, intelligent employer.

Willey, Margaret. *Finding David
  Dolores.* 1986. New York:
  Harper (0–06–026484–5).
  Ages 12–15.

Uncomfortable with the fact that she's
growing up, 13-year-old Arly finds purpose
for her life the day she sees David Dolores.
Then Arly's sophisticated, outgoing friend
Regina manages to get the girls into the
Dolores household, and Arly has to confront her crush face-to-face.

Williams-Garcia, Rita. *Fast Talk
  on a Slow Track.* 1991.
  Dutton/Lodestar (0–525–67334–2).
  Ages 14–18.

Smooth-talking and clever, Denzel Watson
breezes through school and through life until he fails at Princeton's summer program
for minority students. Then a streetwise
dropout introduces him to a fast-track city
life that makes middle-class Denzel question where he really belongs.

Crack, Glue, or a Six-Pack or Two?

WITH GROWING CONCERN ABOUT teenage drug abuse and increased emphasis on drug education in schools, there is no shortage of material on substance abuse (smoking is, perhaps, the exception). The problem is getting teenagers to read books they know are designed to tell them what not to do. Though the following books contain the expected message, the authors avoid outright diatribes, often relying on personal testimony to get their point across in a way that sounds less like a lecture.

"I'm still wild and crazy. I'll swing from a rope over a river. . . . I love fast cars and dangerous amusement park rides. I haven't lost my spirit. But I can never forget that I'm an alcoholic and a drug addict. . . . I won't even be able to have a glass of champagne at my own wedding."
Kimberly, age 16

—from *It Won't Happen to Me*

NONFICTION

Coffey, Wayne. *Straight Talk about Drinking: Teenagers Speak out about Alcohol*. 1988. New York: NAL, paper (0–452–26061–2). Ages 12–17.

Coffey leaves no doubt about his views on alcohol, describing it as a substance that "pollutes" the body and destroys the mind. As the son of an alcoholic, he can testify firsthand to the damage it can cause. He incorporates his own experiences with comments from the medical director of a drug treatment center and some fifty teenagers who have been or are alcohol abusers or who live with an alcoholic family member. He includes facts about the physiological and psychological effects of alcohol as well as insight into why kids drink in the first place, and he explodes a host of common misconceptions about drinking—cold showers, for example, produce clean drunks not sober people. Coffey discusses the dangers of drinking and driving in a separate section, and for teenagers concerned about a friend or parent who's addicted, he explains what "helping by not helping" means.

Cohen, Susan, and Daniel Cohen. *A Six-Pack and a Fake I.D.* 1986. New York: Evans (0–87131–459–2). Ages 13–17.

"The problem is not drinking 'per se,' but drinking too much," write the Cohens who steer clear of preaching against alcohol use and openly criticize those who do. While admitting that alcoholism is a serious problem among youth today, they argue that responsible drinking has a place in everyday social and religious life, as well as a role in a young person's traditional rites of passage. They are clear about alcohol's risks, though, and present facts about its physiological effects and the misconceptions associated with it. They also make a strong case against drinking and driving. Their examples smack of melodrama from time to time, but the informality with which they write makes the reading lively and the information less onerous to absorb.

Cohen, Susan, and Daniel Cohen. *What You Can Believe about Drugs: An Honest and Unhysterical Guide for Teens*. 1988. New York: Evans (0–87131–527–0). Ages 13–17.

The Cohen's give kids more credit for making the right choice about drugs than most books on the subject for teens. By using a congenial, nonstrident approach they hope they get their message across better than "just saying no." Addressing teenagers directly, they examine the fact and fiction associated with a number of frequently abused substances—among them, cocaine, coffee, steroids, and amphetamines. They talk about how drugs work and what they do and explore how attitudes toward various substances have changed over time. The authors openly disapprove of drug testing and their view about marijuana ("for most, the occasional joint is no more dangerous than the occasional beer") is controversial. However, they still take a firm stand against the use of illegal drugs: "don't use 'em."

Harris, Jonathan. *Drugged Athletes: The Crisis in American Sports*. 1987. New York: Macmillan (0–02–742740–4). Ages 12–16.

Harris investgates the scope and pattern of drug abuse in contemporary professional and amateur athletics by combining statistics, profiles of individuals who have won and lost battles with drugs and alcohol, and comments from officials, players, and medical personnel. He includes information on the effects of cocaine, marijuana, and anabolic steroids, along with several other commonly used substances, and looks at how such factors as racial discrimination and violence in sports contribute to drug abuse. He also explores the ongoing controversy over mandatory drug testing. Harris's approach is more informational than self-help, but his book is one of the few that focuses strictly on drug abuse in the sports arena, an area of growing concern today. As such, it may arm kids involved in athletics with enough information to help them make informed choices when competition and pressure become high.

Leite, Evelyn, and Pamela Espeland. *Different Like Me: A Book for Teens Who Worry about Their Parents' Use of Alcohol/Drugs.* 1987. Minneapolis: Johnson Institute, paper (0–935908–34–X). Ages 12–18.

Addressed directly to teenagers who have a substance abuser in their family, this amalgamation of common sense, support, and basic fact comes packaged in a format that sets it apart from much of the teenage material published on the subject. A spacious layout and cartoon drawings invite readers, while concisely written text (rarely more than a paragraph or two) under boldfaced headings introduces information about chemical dependency and its impact on family relationships and personal development. Representative teen responses provide emotional balance. Emphasizing that chemical dependency is an illness, the authors present ideas teens can use to cope with difficult situations at home, suggest healthy ways to vent anger, and explain how such techniques as positive self-talk and prayer can preserve self-esteem. While this is unquestionably a simplistic approach to a complex concern, there's no technical or medical jargon to detract from the message, and the browsable format and sure tone provide just the encouragement some teens need to begin taking care of themselves.

McFarland, Rhoda. *Coping with Substance Abuse.* 1988. New York: Rosen (0–8239–0733–3). Ages 12–16.

A substance abuse counselor draws on her expertise and on fictionalized case histories to explain what happens in families where a member is chemically dependent. Beginning with a questionnaire, "Is There a Drinking Problem in Your Family," McFarland looks first at alcoholism, which she considers a treatable disease. Dramatic vignettes depict how family members of abusers become codependent by denying the abuse, then by covering up the problem and making excuses for the abuser. She urges teens who recognize such family patterns to seek outside help, suggesting further resource material and several organizations they can contact for help. In her section on drugs, she again warns young people not to play rescuer-saver-fixer roles with parents, siblings, or friends who are users. McFarland's style is brisk and animated, but the format of her book is dull and uninviting.

"In rehab a miracle happened. For the first time I started listening to people. When they talked about living I really tuned in. I wanted to live so badly." Cindy

—from *On the Mend*

McMillan, Daniel. *Winning the Battle Against Drugs: Rehabilitation Programs.* 1991. New York: Watts (0–531–11063–X). Ages 14–18.

In the strict sense, McMillan's book is not a self-help text. It doesn't attempt to promote self-esteem or prepare readers to cope practically with their struggle against drug abuse. What it does do is analyze the basic philosophies of drug rehabilitation by zeroing in on different types of treatment centers. McMillan reviews the programs at a comprehensive rehab endeavor that offers both inpatient and outreach service, an adolescent residential program, a Narcotics Anonymous outpatient group, and a methadone maintenance clinic. He also explores the success of various treatments and the controversy surrounding their use—in particular the use of methadone. There are no case studies or personal perspectives to humanize the facts here, but the author's writing style is forceful, direct, and without jargon. Readers in search of general information about programs available, whether for themselves, a friend, or a family member, will discover much of value. McMillan's selective state-by-state listing of drug rehabilitation facilities will be of help as well.

Newman, Susan. *It Won't Happen to Me.* 1987. New York: Putnam/Perigee, paper (0–399–51342–6). Ages 11–14.

In compelling first-person narratives, nine young alcoholics and drug addicts frankly discuss how they became abusers. Newman introduces them briefly, then provides follow-up material consisting of facts about drugs and alcohol and "Think About" sections that probe more philosophical issues—the rationale behind drug use or what to do if a friend drinks or uses drugs, for example. Personal testimonies are the heart of the book, and the many black-and-white photographs will attract browsers. Unfortunately, Newman provides no information on her editorial role, making it difficult to tell whether the narratives are actual speakers' words, and some of the photos are obviously staged and not clearly labeled. Even so, few books containing personal narratives from substance abusers are available for this age level, and that makes Newman's text particularly valuable despite its problems.

Newman, Susan. *You Can Say No to a Drink or a Drug.* 1986. New York: Putnam/Perigee, paper (0–399–51228–4). Ages 11–14.

Endeavoring to guide young people away from substance abuse as she does in her previously discussed book, Newman has devised ten situations in which kids must choose whether or not to use drugs or alcohol. The young people all manage to say no, even in the face of extraordinary pressure from friends or acquaintances. The story circumstances, illustrated with photographs, are generally authentic—the temptation of beer at a friend's slumber party, the dilemma of riding with a friend's older sibling who is obviously drunk. The resolutions are less so; they are even occasionally overdramatic. Still, this book has a message hard to fault, and kids who need practical guidance and support when it comes to facing pressure about drugs may well find it here. Photographs add interest to the presentations, and Newman follows each scenario with a selection of facts and additional insights.

Rosenberg, Maxine B. *Not in My Family: The Truth about Alcoholism.* 1988. New York: Bradbury (0–02–777911–4). Ages 11–14.

Including accounts of eight children and six adults, four of whom were members of ACOA (Adult Children of Alcoholics) at the time of their interviews, Rosenberg exposes the common threads that unite the children of alcoholics, regardless of age. In 14 separate chapters she introduces her subjects, who range in age from 7 to 45. Their individual comments provide the backbone of the quiet but compassionate text, which outlines not only the circumstances of the individuals' lives but also their feelings and coping strategies. As is the case with most of Rosenberg's books, readers in search of hard facts about abuse won't find much here. Instead, Rosenberg concentrates on the effects of the problem on real people and makes it plain that alcoholism isn't always something that "affects the other guy."

Rosenberg, Maxine B. *On the Mend: Getting Away from Drugs.* 1991. New York: Bradbury (0–02–7779141–9). Ages 14–18.

Though Rosenberg once again bases her text on personal interviews, her format for presenting them is different than it was in *Not My Family.* Instead of devoting a chapter to each individual, she combines the stories in this book, running them together in confusing topical chapters that track the teens from their initial involvement with drugs through their crises, their counseling, and their struggles to stay "clean." Her subjects are not as diverse a group as she's chosen in the past; there are no adult perspectives, and the author admits to being "selective in both language and detail." But her book is a frankly spoken record, and the kids, who do most of the speaking (Rosenberg fills in some background), do eventually emerge as compelling distinct examples of the damage drugs can do. An afterword brings the individuals' stories up-to-date. Most, but not all, end successfully.

Ryan, Elizabeth. *Straight Talk about Drugs and Alcohol.* 1989. New York: Facts On File (0–8160–1525–2). Ages 14–18.

Ryan is forceful but not preachy in this book that combines information with earnest advice. A look at the confusing messages about drugs young people receive from the media and from adults comes first. Then Ryan turns to statistics. In separate chapters she details the negative impact alcohol and commonly abused hard drugs have on the body. Coping strategies adapted from Al-Anon's guide to family members of alcoholics are included in a discussion of the impact of substance abuse on family relationships, and sample quizzes from Alateen, Al-Anon, and a variety of other sources allow teenage readers to determine if they have an addiction problem of their own. Ryan urges young people to seek help if they need it and supplies an extensive list of facilities that treat teenage substance abusers.

Shuker, Nancy. *Everything You Need to Know about an Alcoholic Parent.* 1989. New York: Rosen (0–8239–1011–3). Ages 12–15.

In a simplified but effective presentation, Shuker makes readers aware of the codependency trap they face if they have an alcoholic parent. Part of the Need To Know Library series, the book is designed with reluctant readers in mind, its easy-to-read text appealing to teens who dislike books or simply don't read very well. Its information is basic and brief but sufficient to supply readers with an idea of how alcoholism affects family relationships and what can be done to improve things at home, even when an alcoholic parent is unwilling or unable to get help.

Teens Talk about Alcohol and Alcoholism. Students from Mount Anthony Union Junior High School in Bennington, Vermont. Ed. by Paul Dolmetsch and Gail Mauricette. 1987. New York: Doubleday, paper (0–385–23082–0). Ages 11–15.

Alcoholism: the problem may be personal; it may be a parent's; it may be a friend's. Young people involved in a project undertaken by a group of junior high students talk candidly about how alcoholism affected their lives. Scattered through the remarks is solid advice about how to deal with substance abusers and how to help them work toward positive changes that will improve family relationships. A list of resource agencies, such as Al-Anon and Alateen would have been helpful. Teachers will find that the book contains much to prompt classroom discussions, and they'll like its notes on related fiction titles.

FICTION

Brooks, Bruce. *No Kidding.* 1989. New York: Harper (0–06–020722–1); paper (0–06–447051–2). Ages 13–16.

Guardian of his younger brother, 14-year-old Sam is the consummate byproduct of a twenty-first century where rampant alcoholism has caused the collapse of traditional society and children are educated to become the custodians of their families and their futures.

Cadnum, Michael. *Calling Home.* 1991. New York: Viking (0–670–83566–8). Ages 14–18.

Peter is horrified when he kills his best friend in a drunken brawl. He tries to hide his secret by slipping further into alcoholic oblivion.

Childress, Alice. *A Hero Ain't Nothin' but a Sandwich.* 1973. New York: Avon, paper (0–380–00132–2). Ages 14–16.

Benjie Johnson, 13 years old, is a heroin addict. He thinks he can break his habit whenever he wants. When he's forced to try, he discovers it's not as easy as he thought.

Conrad, Pam. *Taking the Ferry Home.* 1988. New York: Harper (0–06–021317–5); paper (0–06–447011–3). Ages 14–18.

Ali Mintz wants sun, fun, and maybe a summer romance with a gorgeous guy. Instead, she finds haughty Simone Silver, whose polish and brashness are merely a cover for feelings about her mother's alcoholism.

Fox, Paula. *The Moonlight Man.* 1986. New York: Bradbury (0–02–735480–6); Dell, paper (0–440–20079–2). Ages 14–18.

When Catherine finally gets an opportunity to spend time alone with her father after her parents' divorce, she discovers that the man she's always idealized is dashing, intelligent, and charming—but only when he's sober.

Miklowitz, Gloria. *Anything to Win.* 1989. New York: Delacorte (0–385–29750–5); Dell, paper (0–440–20732–0). Ages 14–18.

Cam Potter has a chance at a big college scholarship if he puts on 30 pounds. Ignoring health warnings, he starts on steroids to bulk up quickly. It takes rejection by his girlfriend and the death of a longtime steroid user he knows well to shake him out of his destructive pattern.

Strasser, Todd. *The Accident.* 1988. New York: Delacorte (0–440–50061–3); Dell, paper (0–440–20635–9). Ages 12–16.

Even though jocks don't usually mix with burnouts, Matt Thompson and Chris Walsh, who spends most of his time hung over or in trouble, are still friends of a sort. So when Chris is posthumously blamed for the drunk driving accident that caused his death and the death of three others, Matt feels responsible for making certain that what everyone is saying about Chris is actually true.

Private Property: Don't Touch!

RAPE, INCEST, AND PHYSICAL VIOLENCE, once forbidden topics in young adult books, appeared first in teenage fiction. Richard Peck's 1976 novel about a teenage rape victim, *Are You in the House Alone?,* and Fran Arrick's *Steffie Can't Come Out to Play,* about a girl who runs away and becomes a prostitute, led the way. Nonfiction has followed suit, though fiction is still the most common format for dealing with the topics. Girls are the focal point of most of the available material, but there are now a few novels about young men who've been abused, and teenage boys can find facts and support in books such as Benedict's *Safe, Strong, and Streetwise.* Equally apparent is the dearth of preteen material on physical violence and sexual abuse. Children ages 10 to 12, most at risk for abuse according to many sources consulted during preparation of this chapter, have few books to turn to. Hopefully, publishers soon will begin to address this concern.

"It wasn't sexual assault . . . we were just taking advantage of a girl who was there." Kevin, age 15

—from *Voices of Rape*

NONFICTION

Benedict, Helen. *Safe, Strong, and Streetwise.* 1987. Boston: Joy Street Books/Little, Brown (0–316–08900–4). Ages 12–18.

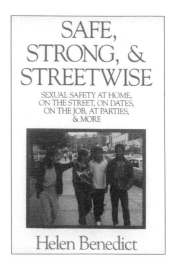

A rape crisis counselor discusses sexual assault and explains how teenagers can prepare for, protect against, and deal with it should it occur. Statements from victims add immediacy to the text, which emphasizes that "awareness and escape," not physical defense methods, are the most important factors in self-protection. Benedict goes further than most authors who write about sexual assault by recognizing the concerns of male victims, and she provides sound guideposts for young people of both sexes who may be confused by sexually exploitive situations on dates, on the job, or at school. Sensitive, explicit, and practical, the book is dedicated to helping teenagers survive in a world where, Benedict feels, personal safety can no longer be taken for granted.

Bode, Janet. *Voices of Rape.* 1990. New York: Watts (0–531–15184–0). Ages 14–18.

A rapist, a police officer, a rape survivor, and a defense attorney are among the people who speak out on a sensitive subject that is rarely presented as candidly in books for young adults as it is here. Young people speak out frankly: "We're not just a two legged penis," insists one young man, involved in a discussion Bode orchestrated in a ninth-grade classroom. Professionals are equally forthright. Dr. Judith Becker, director of a juvenile sex offender treatment program, voices strong concern about violence in contemporary society and talks openly about aberrant sexual behavior, addressing some of her comments directly to teenage boys; a nurse explains what attack victims experience in the hospital; a veteran police officer discusses procedures used by the sex crimes unit of a large metropolitan police department. Bode also includes some voices of an different sort: a boy who's convinced that what he did wasn't rape and a victim of date rape who admits she is still attracted to her attacker. Then the author takes the speaker's platform for herself, first addressing males, then females, then both on how to stop the crime. As an assault survivor and a rape crisis worker, Bode knows the issues, and she describes them extremely well.

Janet Bode Tackles Tough Subjects

An enthusiastic speaker and writer, totally dedicated to her audience, Janet Bode routinely tackles tough, important issues. Rape is one of them, and Bode was one of the first to write about it for teenagers. In fact, her own survival of a vicious attack started her on a writing career that has lasted more than 15 years. "We use the expression 'I'm going to write a book about it,'" she says. "I did." It was a book for the adult trade market. But writing for adults, which she continues to do, was not enough. A former secondary school teacher, Bode felt a strong affinity for teenagers, and she believed she had something important to tell them. *Rape,* her first young adult book, was published in 1979. It is still in print. She calls *Voices of Rape,* published in 1990, its update. Actually, it is a great deal more than a new edition. It's a book about individuals, not about statistics, and how Bode wrote it is as fascinating as the book itself.

SZ: How do you go about finding teenagers to interview, especially when you're going to ask questions about a subject like rape?

JB: I ask a school's permission. Then after I speak to a group, I say, "if any of you students would ever be interested in having me interview you for one of my books, please put down your name and phone number and write a line about yourself." Lots of kids will do that. Librarians are another source. I impose on them. I explain who I am and what project I'm dealing with, and I ask if there's a student or students they feel would be good for me to interview.

I speak with many more people than I include in my books. I select the ones that I feel will best reflect a body of information or express a point of view. I felt it was important in *Voices of Rape,* for example, to include Kevin, who participated in the gang rape, and a young woman who went through a date rape because, I'm sad to say, they were representative and typical.

SZ: Do your visits to schools generate ideas for new books as well as potential interview subjects?

JB: Yes. Students are my best resource. I remember this teenage boy sitting back in the library, leaning back in his chair . . . I was sure he was going to fall over . . . but he raised his hand and said, "I *hate* my brothers and sisters. You ought to write a book on that." So I did. *[Truce: Ending the Sibling War]* The same thing led to *Different Worlds,* my book about interracial and cross-cultural dating.

SZ: How do you get teenagers to feel enough at ease to talk openly?

JB: I think that one of the lucky talents I have is to get teenagers to open up honestly. Some interviews I do face to face. Often I do phone interviews because I talk to kids across the country. They know the rules ahead of time: I will change their name and the fine details of their identity to protect their privacy. There has to be some type of general conversation first. They don't immediately sit down and say, "Let me tell you about this terrible experience that happened to me." I may ask something like, "Describe the room where you're sitting right now." They can talk a little about that room, and sometimes I'll tell them I live in New York City, and I'm sitting at my desk, and I can look out the window and see the Empire State Building. They like that. It gives them a little definition of who I am.

What always impresses me is that teenagers take the interview very seriously. They clean up their language; there are not many swear words in what they tell me, because they're being listened to. They know they have a chance to help other people who might have been in a similar situation. They really are quite wonderful.

SZ: How do you manage to capture the individuality of the people you interview?

JB: I work very hard to preserve the spirit of what people say. I take out some of the "likes" and "you knows." I do leave some in, because it's important for me to use each teenager's words and idiomatic expressions. And I listen. A little bell goes off, a *"wow,* that's a great way to put that," or "that's so important," or "that really moved me," or "that speaks to other teenagers in a way they will really understand." At a certain level, it's just gut instinct.

SZ: It must have been very hard for you, a rape survivor, to write *Voices of Rape.*

JB: Yes. I thought it had been a long enough time. Time does make a difference, and I felt I had learned and grown from my experience. But *Voices of Rape* ended up being a difficult book to do. It brought back more memories than I wanted. I didn't want to have to start thinking about that stuff again; I didn't want to have to go to a police station or to start thinking in the way that I do when I write. I get totally involved in my topics. But I think that teenagers deserve the best books I can possibly write; they deserve the most interesting people I can possibly interview. That's why I interviewed a famous defense attorney named Barry Slotnick. He was the lawyer who handled the trial of Bernie Goetz, New York City's subway gunman. I thought Slotnick was an articulate, quotable man. If I were doing a book for adults, that's who I'd interview, so that's who I talked with for *Voices of Rape.*

SZ: Slotnick talked about defending rapists in court. You probably didn't like what he had to say, but it certainly didn't show in your book.

JB: You're right. I had to control myself; I wanted to jump across the room at him. When I described him in the book I wanted to use adjectives that weren't very nice.

SZ: Do you think boys will read *Voices?*

JB: Well, boys aren't the traditional audience for this kind of book. When I envision my audience I see many more 15-year-old girls than I do boys. But I think we *expect* that. I hope teenage males will pick it up. If a boy reads the chapter by Dr. Judith Becker, an expert on juvenile sex offenders, and sees that he's doing things that might lead to difficulties . . . it's the old teacher in me. If I can just change one person, my whole job is worthwhile.

SZ: Your first book about rape for teenagers came out in 1979. Have attitudes changed over the decade between the publication of that book and *Voices?*

JB: I think a few things have changed in 10 years, but not enough. I believe much more can be done. I am a little concerned now that women are becoming subservient again in some ways, and that troubles me. I have seen improvement with the police. Now some police forces are required to take sensitivity training. That was something those of us who worked in the rape crisis centers only dreamed of happening. When you go into a hospital in a major city now, people are much more considerate than they were when I did the last book. Back then they'd often scream out, "Rape victim, come in,". . . just what you didn't want. Laws have changed, too. Today, the sexual history of the woman on the stand testifying cannot be examined. I think that is a tremendous improvement, even though, in some cases, attorneys still manage to bring it up.

SZ: *Voices* is an extremely forthright book. Dr. Becker, for example, speaks very candidly about violent sexual behavior in teenage boys. Do you think *Voices* is going to become a target of the censors?

JB: Judith Becker even asked about that when I spoke with her. It may. But I think knowledge *is* power, and only through listening and reading and beginning to think about information can we deal with topics like this. When I talk to kids, they agree that you don't solve problems by ignoring them or by not being willing to discuss them. You have to get the high intensity light out. You have to look at them, discuss them. And you have to deal with them in order to become better and strong and end this horrible thing called rape.

———————————

Cooney, Judith. *Coping with Sexual Abuse.* 1987. New York: Rosen (0–8239–0684–1); paper (0–8239–0763–5). Ages 14–18.

Cooney, a Professor in the Division of Psychology and Counseling at Governors State University in Illinois, contributes a tough, explicit discussion of incest and sexual abuse. In brisk, no-nonsense fashion she explodes myths associated with abuse, explains how adults misuse power and authority to trap victims, and looks at the effects abuse has on all concerned. Tightly organized, with chapter summaries and lists of topics for discussion, her book is more textbook than self-help manual. But Cooney does speak straight to readers in her final section, urging them to reveal abuse and break the vicious cycle of pain, despite the family and personal trauma that is likely to follow.

Daugherty, Lynn. *Why Me? Help for Victims of Child Sexual Abuse (Even if They Are Adults Now).* 1984. Racine, Wis.: Mother Courage Press, paper (0–941300–01–3). Ages 14–up.

In a book published for adults but filled with information of value to teenage survivors as well, Daugherty deals with the psychological aftermath of child sexual abuse. Victims, many of them young people, describe their experiences in plain-spoken words: Tina explains how she, at age 13, was grabbed by a rapist as she walked along the road; Greg, now age 20, recalls how he was raped when he spent the night in a juvenile detention center; and Jessica, age 4, remembers being taken from home after it was discovered she was being abused by her older brother. To help dispel the confusion victims feel about their experience, Daugherty supplies facts in a question/answer section. She then turns to the psychological stages that follow traumatic events and identifies specific feelings survivors have, from anger to fear to guilt. The author is convinced that survivors can do much on their own to begin the difficult process of healing. But as a psychologist who works with abused children and adults, she also knows the importance of outside help and explains how to choose a therapist in a concluding section.

Kosof, Anna. *Incest: Families in Crisis.* 1985. New York: Watts (0–531–10071–5). Ages 14–18.

More informational than self-help in orientation, this is nonetheless an important discussion of a topic about which little specifically written for teenagers exists. Kosof, who concentrates mainly on father-daughter incest, reveals what researchers have discovered about the crime and reflects on the psychological ramifications the act has on those who have suffered. Viewing incest as a family tragedy involving both parents to some extent, she discusses the distorted relationship between child and mother as well as between father and daughter. She clearly shows the conflicts associated with bringing the crime into the open and writes candidly about the ordeal that can follow, which may include years of therapy and a breakup of the family. Poignant words of survivors and comments from offenders appear throughout the text, which is frank and enlightening without ever becoming sensational. Kosof's own anger at the situation comes through.

Kyte, Kathy S. *Play It Safe: The Kids' Guide to Personal Safety and Crime Prevention.* 1983. New York: Knopf (0–394–95964–7). Ages 11–14.

Kyte assembles some familiar but solid advice on self-protection and packages it in a format that should attract kids who like to browse the shelves as well as kids in search of help and information. She introduces her subject with fictional portraits of victims and general advice on how not to become one. Follow-up chapters suggest sensible safety tips to use at school, at home, and on public transportation and provide advice on rape prevention and how to deal with abuse by a parent. The counsel is more than a series of do's and don'ts; Kyte makes the reasoning behind her words very clear. A multiple-choice test helps readers gauge their safety awareness, and cartoon drawings add visual appeal, an important factor in catching kids' attention. With little else for the age group available on the subject, this title, though old, is still an important resource.

> "Whatever else, you feel you want to love your parents. It's amazing how strongly you want to excuse them, protect them, take the blame for what happened."
>
> —from *Incest*

Mufson, Susan, and Rachel Kranz. *Straight Talk about Child Abuse.* 1991. New York: Facts On File (0–8160–2376–X). Ages 12–18.

While the dust jacket shouts "textbook," this cooperative effort by a free-lance writer and a certified social worker will be as valuable to teenagers needing advice on how to cope with a problem at home as it will to those looking for report material. Part of the Straight Talk series, the book defines and discusses both physical and emotional abuse. It focuses, in particular, on abuse within the family and presents a clear idea of the consequences abuse leaves in its wake. Going further than most writers who deal with the subject for a teenage audience, Mufson and Kranz link child abuse to substance abuse and explain the complicated dynamics that make it possible for victims to love their abusers and blame themselves for what's not their fault. The authors are frank about what can happen when abuse is brought into the open—foster care, possibly family dissolution—but they strongly encourage teens to do what's necessary to alter the pattern. Profiles of teenage victims provide signposts for recognizing abusive situations.

Parrot, Andrea. *Coping with Date Rape & Acquaintance Rape.* 1988. New York: Rosen (0–8239–0784–8); paper (0–8239–0808–9). Ages 14–18.

Dr. Parrot, on the faculty of Cornell University, is a specialist in human sexuality and rape prevention. She contends that though an individual may make her- or himself vulnerable to attack (by drinking too much, for example), forced sex or sex performed because of threats is a criminal act that is not the fault of the victim. Explicit examples of date rape situations help her clarify the nature of the crime and define the legal, social, and emotional misconceptions and prejudices associated with it. Her discussion of popular myths, specific behaviors, and sex-role stereotypes contributing to the "date rape dynamic" focuses largely on women victims, but she also includes an excellent section on the special problems male victims face. The book's format is dull, but Parrot's forthright, sobering text puts to rest a number of widely held misconceptions. In addition, it presents a few sensible self-protection strategies and provides information on where to get help if rape occurs.

Rue, Nancy N. *Coping with Dating Violence.* 1989. New York: Rosen (0–8239–0997–2). Ages 14–18.

Abuse is not the fault of the victim, despite myths about young women who "bring it on themselves" and boys who are merely "being boys." That's the overriding message Rue, a free-lance writer, delivers in a book targeted at teenage girls. Dramatic case histories demonstrate typical situations that occur, and guidelines for avoiding assault are direct and practical. Rue also supplies checklists identifying warning signals and abuse patterns and discusses why boys become abusers and why girls often quietly accept violation. She writes about getting help, too, emphasizing that victims can't change abusers, who must secure professional counseling. Sources are documented in chapter notes.

Shuker-Haines, Frances. *Everything You Need to Know about Date Rape.* 1989. New York: Rosen (0–8239–1013–X). Ages 12–16.

Though amateurish, photographs add drama to a book that begins by chastising the media for encouraging stereotypes of women as objects. Using a simple fictional scenario, Shuker-Haines then demonstrates what can and often does happen during date rape and suggests several things that might help someone keep an uncomfortable situation from getting totally out of control. She touches briefly on related

medical, legal, and cultural issues, but her main concern is exposing misconceptions about the act. Boys take the brunt of her criticism, though she does include a chapter about young men as victims and strongly cautions young women about teasing and other misleading behaviors. Part of the Need To Know series, this easy-to-read book is a competent, simplified overview. Though published for reluctant readers, it may be of use to others as well.

Warshaw, Robin. *I Never Called It Rape.* 1988. New York: Harper (0–06–055126–7); paper (0–06–096276–3). Ages 15–up.

"Unknown, denied, or ignored by most people," acquaintance rape is one of the least understood physical assaults. To demonstrate the enormity of the problem and educate readers on assault prevention, journalist Warshaw draws on the findings of a nationwide study of undergraduate college women conducted by *Ms.* magazine under the auspices of the National Institute of Mental Health. Filled with survey statistics and explicit first-hand accounts, including some testimony that recalls events that took place during teen years, Warshaw's dramatically written summary of the survey's findings supplies a wealth of information on a subject of great import to young women today.

FICTION

Byars, Betsy. *Cracker Jackson.* 1985. New York: Viking/Kestrel (0–670–80546–7). Ages 11–14.

Eleven-year-old Cracker Jackson loves his babysitter Alma, but he's certain her husband beats her. His endeavors to convince her to get help for herself and her baby lead to unexpected and tragic consequences.

Geller, Mark. *Raymond.* 1988. New York: Harper/Charlotte Zolotow (0–06–022206–9). Ages 11–14.

When bruises from his father's most recent beating come to the attention of a gym teacher who reports the incident to the authorities, Raymond faces his angry father anew. This time, however, he fights back, then runs away.

Honeycutt, Natalie. *Ask Me Something Easy.* 1991. New York: Watts/Orchard/Richard Jackson (0–531–05894–8). Ages 12–15.

At age 17, Addie looks back to the days after her father abandoned the family and she became the scapegoat for her mother's rage and abuse.

Irwin, Hadley. *Abby, My Love.* 1985. New York: Atheneum/Margaret K. McElderry (0–689–50323–7). Ages 14–16.

Chip has known Abby since they were both children. But it's not until the pair is in high school that Chip finds out his clever, sensitive girlfriend has been sexually abused by her father for years.

Maclean, John. *Mac.* 1987. New York: Houghton (0–395–43080–1). Ages 14–18.

A good friend, a competent student, and a generally nice guy, high school sophomore Mac has grown up trusting and secure. Then he's assaulted by a doctor during a physical exam and his world turns upside down.

Martin, Katherine. *Night Riding.* 1989. New York: Knopf (0–679–80064–6). Ages 13–15.

Prin Campbell's growing friendship with lonely Mary Faith, the 15-year-old pregnant teenager who has moved in next door, leads to the discovery that the father and grandfather of Mary Faith's baby are one and the same.

Mazer, Norma Fox. *Silver.* 1988. New York: Morrow (0–688–06865–0). Ages 12–15.

Sarabeth becomes privy to an awful secret: her well-to-do friend Patty Lewis is being sexually molested by her uncle.

Miklowitz, Gloria. *Secrets Not Meant to Be Kept.* 1987. New York: Delacorte (0–385–29491–3). Ages 14–18.

Sixteen-year-old Adri has never communicated well with her parents. In fact, she is unable to handle personal contact of any kind; she dislikes being hugged or kissed even by her mother. Now the innocent kisses of a boy she likes and her young sister's strange behavior have triggered visions of herself as a child in pain, cold, and desperately afraid. Is she losing her mind?

Talbert, Marc. *The Paper Knife.* 1989. New York: Dial (0–8037–0571–9). Ages 11–14.

Unable to admit to anyone that he was sexually abused by his mother's boyfriend, 10-year-old Jeremy is glad when he and his mother move to another town. Then a misunderstanding occurs and his new teacher, Mr. Williams, is wrongfully accused of the crime.

Weinstein, Nina. *No More Secrets.* 1991. Seattle, Wash.: Seal Press (1–878067–07–9); paper (1–878067–00–1). Ages 14–18.

Attacked at the age of 8 by a stranger who came to her room while her mother was elsewhere in the house, Mandy has never been able to admit she was actually raped. Now, at age 16, she finds the stress of the long-held secret more than she can bear.

Wellness

ONE OF THE MOST interesting developments in health-related materials for young people is the proliferation of books focusing on emotional and psychological issues. Topics such as stress, depression, and anorexia, not long ago thought totally inappropriate for "impressionable" teenagers, are being written about and discussed more openly than ever before. But as with books on sexuality, their use still engenders controversy, the concern being whether teenagers will accept the advice in books as a substitute for the professional counseling they may need. Although it's impossible to say how individuals will react to the books they read (fiction, for example, may have greater impact than fact), most responsible treatments of these subjects make it plain to the reader that an author's advice (even when the author is a medical practitioner) is not the equivalent of a personal physician's care.

Publishers have been less responsive to teenagers' physical problems, in some instances, than to their mental health concerns. For example, there are virtually no books for teenagers who suffer from allergies, a common complaint. There are still

---

"My brother saw the movie *Ghostbusters* and told me that I was like Sigourney Weaver in the film. He said I'd been invaded by a powerful demon like she was supposed to have been, and that mine was anorexia." Larrayne, age 16
　　　　　　　　　　　　　　　—from *When Food's a Foe*

---

a number of useful physical-health-related titles, however. The ones that follow range from practical guidebooks on skin care to inspiring stories of kids whose lives are full despite serious physical problems.

NONFICTION

Too Fat or Too Thin?

Erlanger, Ellen. *Eating Disorders: A Question and Answer Book about Anorexia Nervosa and Bulimia Nervosa.* 1988. Minneapolis: Lerner (0-8225-0038-8). Ages 11–15.

Erlanger wants to alert young people to the symptoms of eating disorders so they can recognize their own problem or secure help for a friend whom they suspect is a sufferer. To accomplish that goal, she devotes initial chapters to characteristics generally associated with anorexia and bulimia. She follows up with first-person accounts of two individuals who have overcome eating disorders, supplying a close-up look at how the illnesses affect not only health and emotional well-being but also relationships with family and friends. A helpful bibliography, which includes a selection of audiovisual materials, provides direction for those who wish to pursue the subject in more detail.

Kane, June Kozak. *Coping with Diet Fads.* 1990. New York: Rosen (0-8239-1005-9). Ages 12–16.

Bombarded by messages that "thin is in," teenagers are more than a little concerned about being overweight. A dietitian who specializes in obesity in young people, Kane knows the right ways and wrong ways to trim off the pounds. After stressing that a visit to a nutritionist or a physician is a good first step in any weight-loss plan, she furnishes teenagers with solid nutritional advice and good sense about diet fads. Teenagers looking for menu planning help won't find much here. Kane's more concerned with the connection between food and feelings and supplying

information that will help teenagers develop healthy attitudes toward food that will last a lifetime.

Kolodny, Nancy J. *When Food's a Foe: How to Confront and Conquer Eating Disorders.* 1992. Rev. ed. Boston: Little, Brown, paper (0–316–50181–6). Ages 14–18.

Questions and awareness activities are the heart of this book that revolves around the idea that sufferers of eating disorders can do much to help themselves if they admit their illness, find out about it, and take positive action to control it. Kolodny, head

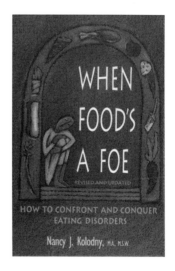

of a behavior-modification eating-disorders program in Connecticut, prefaces the practical part of her text with solid background on anorexia and bulimia and a thought-provoking analysis of the link between body image and self-esteem. Then, through combined use of charts, insightful questions, and straightforward discussion, she helps readers pinpoint self-destructive patterns and diffuse the "negative triggers" that make food a destructive force in their lives. Her text is both positive and realistic. Kolodny never pretends getting well will be easy or that her suggestions will work for everyone. In fact, she includes an excellent chapter about avenues of extra help for teens who acknowledge they can't go it alone.

Landau, Elaine. *Weight: A Teenage Concern.* 1991. New York: Dutton/ Lodestar (0–525–67335–0). Ages 12–17.

The embarrassments and prejudices associated with being overweight reverberate through the comments of many of the teens who tell their stories here. Landau sets their accounts in perspective, adding information about what causes obesity, how fatness is related to anorexia nervosa and bulimia, what society thinks about "heavyweights," and the kinds of weight-loss methods available today. She goes several steps further than most teenage books on the subject by including testimonies of teens who have come to terms with their extra-large size. She also takes a quick look at how organizations like NAAFA, the National Association to Advance Fat Acceptance, promote self-pride and fight discrimination.

Lukes, Bonnie L. *How to Be a Reasonably Thin Teenage Girl: Without Starving, Losing Your Friends, or Running Away from Home.* 1986. New York: Atheneum (0–689–31269–5). Ages 11–14.

Lukes's style is flip, but that doesn't interfere with her practical advice. An "ex-fatty," she knows all about dieters' woes and the temptations that face the overweight. Grounded in her own experience, her suggestions for handling everything from family dinners to special occasions where food is served pivot around sensible, well-balanced eating. Lukes knows, too, about reasonable goal setting. She advises readers not to try to lose more than a pound or so a week and not to set their overall weight loss goals too high. The book contains little on eating disorders and not enough about why people overeat, but Lukes's breezy style and good humor are refreshing. Teens seriously concerned about weight management in today's "spaghetti—cream-sauced—french-fried world" will find that Lukes presents some excellent tips for handling daily dieting challenges. Cartoon drawings are well-paired to the narrative.

Maloney, Michael, and Rachel Kranz. *Straight Talk about Eating Disorders.* 1991. New York: Facts On File (0–06–021641–7). Ages 14–18.

A doctor and a free-lance writer inform readers about the three best-known eating disorders—anorexia nervosa, bulimia, and compulsive eating. They deal first with society's mixed messages about weight and body image and lay out the basic facts about eating patterns. It's their use of composite, cause-and-effect case studies that distinguish their book. Young adults will need to keep in mind that things are more complicated in real life than they are in these studies, but the intriguing scenarios depict the psychological underpinnings of the illnesses in a way that's bound to sharpen understanding and make it easier for teens to remember the factual information the book supplies.

Moe, Barbara. *Coping with Eating Disorders.* 1991. New York: Rosen (0–8239–1343–0). Ages 12–16.

While *Straight Talk about Eating Disorders* by Maloney and Kranz, above, is more comprehensive as well as more specific about the health consequences involved, Moe covers some of the same ground in a book with a much more appealing format. Without probing deeply, she discusses the characteristics of each of the three major eating disorders—bulimia, anorexia, and compulsive eating—and examines the impact of the media on our weight conscious culture and how eating disorders arise as a result of family dysfunction. Numerous authentic-sounding thumbnail profiles provide a strong sense of the dangers of destructive eating. Sensible goals for teens ready to confront their illness and a solid selection of follow-up resources round out the book.

Salter, Charles A. *Looking Good, Eating Right: A Sensible Guide to Proper Nutrition and Weight Loss for Teens.* 1991. Brookfield, Conn.: Millbrook (1–56294–047–3). Ages 12–15.

Learning to eat right takes information as well as self-discipline. Salter provides the former while giving teens plenty of encouragement and excellent reasons to invoke the latter. He includes helpful insights into fads and eating disorders, though the majority of the book is devoted to outlining the basic principles of healthy eating and weight control, which he presents in a pleasant conversational tone. Chapters describe sensible, age-appropriate ways to lose weight, including brief exercise guidelines. A final section is devoted to answering common questions teenagers ask about dieting. For more specific information on eating disorders teens can turn to books by Landau, Maloney and Kranz, or Silverstein, described elsewhere in this section. Salter focuses more on eating "right" than eating "wrong."

Salter, Charles A. *The Vegetarian Teen.* 1991. Brookfield, Conn.: Millbrook (1–56294–048–1). Ages 12–15.

"It is always wise to consult your doctor before changing your diet in a major way" begins an introduction to vegetarianism that is enthusiastic but also considerate of the nutritional needs of teenagers. Salter helps the curious decide whether a vegetarian diet is something they'd like to try and supplies enough background to get them started safely. A question-answer section spotlights common concerns teenagers have about the life-style ("Should I tell dates I'm vegetarian?" "How can I be a vegetarian in the school cafeteria?" "How do I get my parents to go along with my vegetarianism?"), and a selection of simple-to-prepare recipes provides the incentive to begin experiments with new foods right away. Salter does cram a lot of information into this little book (barely 90 pages), but young adults serious about vegetarianism will need still more, especially about maintaining a nutritionally balanced diet. Unfortunately, Salter's list of further readings is too limited to be much help.

Sanchez, Gail Jones, and Mary Gerbino. *Overeating: Let's Talk about It.* 1986. Minneapolis: Dillon, paper (0–87518–319–0). Ages 11–13.

Readers in search of calorie charts won't find them here. Instead of strict diets, the authors promote behavior modification and good nutrition. In part one of their text, they lay out strategies for coping with the emotions that prompt overeating and for dealing with insensitive comments about weight that lower self-esteem. Part two introduces information about nutrition and exercise. Simplified stick-figure illustrations depicting exercise procedures are inadequate, but the shopping tips, vitamin information, and goal-setting guidelines will certainly provide help to young people facing up to weight concerns.

Silverstein, Alvin, and others. *So You Think You're Fat?* 1991. New York: HarperCollins (0–06–021642–5). Ages 12–18.

Compulsive eating, the least publicized of the principal food-abuse disorders, gets full attention in this direct but not overly formal presentation. Consideration of a lengthy list of health problems—from heart disease to depression—related to being overweight leads off, followed by well-amplified discussions of psychological, cultural, and biological factors that contribute to obesity. The authors also take a look at the diet industry and supply a wealth of diet-related miscellany, covering everything from yo-yo dieting to exercise. A few dieter's tips are included, but this is a background book, not a practical weight-loss guide. It's the kind of book that needs to be read before the word "diet" even comes up for discussion.

Physical Challenges

American Diabetes Association.
Diabetes in the Family. Rev. ed.
1987. New York: Prentice-Hall,
paper (0–13–208653–0).
Ages 14–up.

This informative and authoritative source-book, published originally for an adult audience, will be useful to teenagers who must manage diabetes on a day-to-day basis. The text includes basic information about the disease as well as discussions of glucose-tolerance testing, diet, exercise, personal hygiene, and insulin control. It also considers the impact of the illness on such aspects of daily living as travel and the pursuit of a career. Sample meal plans and food-exchange lists are appended.

Bombeck, Erma. *I Want to Grow
Hair, I Want to Grow Up, I
Want to Go to Boise: Children
Surviving Cancer.* 1989. New
York: Harper (0–06–016170–1);
paper (0–06–109905–8).
Ages 14–up.

The syndicated humorist, known for her good-natured pokes at suburbia, left her traditional territory for the more somber realms of a hospital, where she spoke with young cancer patients. There's terrible sadness in her anecdote-laden chapters, which limn kids' reactions to their initial diagnoses, their chemotherapy, and the very real possibility that they might die. But there's also a great deal more than pain and fear. The stories are laced with poignant humor and a surprising optimism that can help cancer victims, friends, and parents better handle the realities of a tragic disease.

Carter, Sharon, and Judy Monnig.
Coping with a Hospital Stay.
1987. New York: Rosen
(0–8239–0682–5). Ages 12–16.

Their clichéd humor ("tell the doctor to cripple that and walk it by you slow") is occasionally distracting, but free-lance writer Carter and Monnig, who is a nurse, still manage to get across some useful tips for teenagers facing hospital confinement. Alert to the emotional turmoil that often accompanies hospitalization, they urge patients to assert themselves by asking questions about their condition and about hospital procedures and bring their feelings out into the open. Their guidelines for such varied concerns as managing with a roommate, keeping up with schoolwork, contending with boredom, and dealing with the "Gloria Glooms" and "Little Mary Sunshines" who visit are practical and sensitive, and the inclusion of a young patient's diary adds a sense of how everything fits together. Though the authors don't ignore the possibility of death, they keep their tone light, cheerful, and encouraging.

"When three-year-old Carrie's blond curls were all gone and a little fuzz was starting to grow back, she observed with curiosity her father's head as he bent to tie his shoe. 'Daddy,' she asked, 'is your hair coming or going?'"
—from *I Want to Grow Hair, I Want to Grow Up, I Want to Go to Boise*

Fine, Judylaine. *Afraid to Ask: A
Book about Cancer.* 1986. New
York: Lothrop (0–688–06195–8);
paper (0–688–06196–6).
Ages 12–17.

A free-lance writer and editor of *Feeling Good,* an educational publication put out by the Canadian Cancer Society, Fine presents a book about cancer that she's written for teenagers and "for families to share." Explaining that there's still a lot about cancer that science doesn't comprehend, she considers what's known about how cancer cells work, who's at risk for the illness, and how patients are treated. In a moving chapter she's titled "Death and Dying," she combines personal accounts with material gleaned from the research of Dr. Elisabeth Kübler-Ross to contribute a sense of what terminally ill patients and their families must endure. The last third of her text looks a little more closely at specific types of cancer, outlining their symptoms and reviewing risk factors, treatment approaches, and survival statistics. Fine seeks to prepare readers for the emotional upheaval a diagnosis of cancer can bring to a family, and, by making the illness more understandable, she's gone a long way toward achieving her goal.

Goodheart, Barbara. *Diabetes*. 1990. New York: Watts (0–531–10882–1). Ages 12–15.

Goodheart's organization and approach make her book more likely to be chosen as curriculum support than as self-help material. Even so, her lucid overview can help diabetics and their family members, as well as students, attain a clearer picture of Type I and Type II diabetes. Her discussions of home and hospital testing and treatment incorporate information on how diet and exercise as well as insulin are used in diabetes management. Although Goodheart maintains that most diabetics who take proper care of themselves can live normal, productive lives, she is honest about the demanding nature of the illness, both on personal relationships and on one's daily routines. She makes the necessity of eating at regular intervals, exercising cautiously, and measuring blood-sugar levels abundantly clear.

Gravelle, Karen, and Bertram A. John. *Teenagers Face to Face with Cancer*. 1986. Englewood Cliffs, N.J.: Messner (0–671–54549–3). Ages 12–17.

It's difficult enough to cope with the changes of adolescence without having to face the extraordinary demands of a life-threatening illness. However, that's just what the sixteen young people profiled in this book must do. Ranging in age from 13 to 21, they all have cancer, and at a time when most of their contemporaries are striving toward independence, they are fighting to stay alive. With Gravelle and Bertram supplying facts and sensitive interpretation, the teenagers speak freely about their conflicting feelings, their treatment, their changing relationships with family and friends, and the stares and insensitive comments, "Hey leukemia boy." Their combined comments coalesce into an affecting record of how illness touches the young—and how adversity can generate emotional strength.

Krementz, Jill. *How It Feels to Fight for Your Life*. 1989. Boston: Little, Brown (0–316–50364–9). Ages 10–15.

As she did in other volumes in her How It Feels series, Krementz ably preserves the individuality of the fourteen young people she interviewed for this affecting collective profile, illustrated with excellent black-and-white photographs. The children, who range in age from 7 to 16, articulately express how they cope with the fear and the pain associated with traumatic conditions such as cystic fibrosis, arthritis, and epilepsy. Their words are unpretentious and never sentimental. Their special strengths and personalities emerge distinctly through their accounts, as do the feelings and interests that bond them with most other children.

Krementz, Jill. *How It Feels to Live with a Physical Disability*. 1992. New York: Simon and Schuster (0–671–72371–5). Ages 10–15.

Of all Krementz's books in the How It Feels series this is, perhaps, the most powerful. It focuses on physically challenged youngsters, profiling twelve whom Krementz talked with and photographed with their families and friends. As always, she presents the interviews as smoothly written, separate first-person narratives, with no obvious editorial intervention. She captures the individual voices and characters of the children beautifully—from blind 13-year-old Ivonne, who uses a laser cane and loves to dance and play the piano, to 16-year-old Francis Smith, abandoned by his parents because they couldn't cope with his severe medical problems. The young people speak about their arduous medical treatment, thoughtfully voice the frustrations of their everyday lives, and talk about their hopes for the future. There's no self-pity in their words. What comes through most vividly is the sense of pride they have in their achievements, whether they're remembering how they made a new friend, tied a shoe, or walked with an artificial leg. Their stories are examples to us all.

Simmons, Richard. *Reach for Fitness: A Special Book of Exercises for the Physically Challenged.* 1986. New York: Warner (0–446–51302–4). Ages 14–up.

A dedicated promoter of fitness familiar to television audiences, Simmons consulted physical therapy experts before pulling together this amalgamation of good-sense nutrition and exercise of interest to physically challenged individuals as well as their families and friends. He includes specific regimens for people coping with cerebral palsy, cystic fibrosis, and spina bifida, as well as a number of other conditions. Illustrations clarify his descriptions, which include reminders to approach exercise sensibly, take appropriate precautions, and set realistic goals.

"To make sure that others like us, we become people pleasers. We would rather be the givers than the takers, whether of compliments, offers of help, or presents. We measure our worth by the people around us. . . . We pick up the pieces for them while our own lives are falling apart."
—from *Coping with Codependency*

Tiger, Steven. *Diabetes.* 1987. Englewood Cliffs, N.J.: Messner (0–671–63272–6). Ages 11–13.

Basic facts about diabetes are introduced in a text supported by an eight-page section of full-color photographs and diagrams. After explaining how the body normally processes food, the author looks at what happens when diabetes is present and explains several different types of the illness. Young people coping with diabetes will find much of interest in the

ensuing discussion of current diagnostic techniques, treatments, and research now underway.

Emotions, Stress, and Mental Illness

Adderholdt-Elliott, Miriam. *Perfectionism: What's Bad About Being Too Good?* 1987. Minneapolis: Free Spirit, paper (0–915793–07–5). Ages 12–16.

An admitted perfectionist, Adderholdt-Elliott blends personal experience with research findings in an informative guide that clearly distinguishes the difference between obsessive perfectionism and the healthy pursuit of excellence. Using an informal style that makes the text easy to read, she explains the detrimental effects the desire to be perfect has on mind, body, and relationships, and explores alternate ways individuals can regain their perspective and still satisfy their desire to succeed. She also talks about finding professional help when it's necessary and discusses how young women can avoid falling victim to the burdens of rapidly changing role expectations. Cartoon drawings lighten the mood.

Buckingham, Robert Wm., and Sandra K. Huggard. *Coping with Grief.* 1991. New York: Rosen (0–8239–1271–X). Ages 12–15.

Although grief is traditionally associated with death, it is also a byproduct of many other situations involving loss and change. Buckingham, "founding father" of the first hospice in America, and Huggard explain how divorce, romantic breakup, and even unexpected teenage pregnancy or the loss of a pet can trigger feelings similar to emotions that follow the death of a loved one. Personal accounts are the backbone of the text. The authors follow each individual's experience with a recap of the story, an evaluation of the feelings expressed, and brief comments about the strategies used to handle the grief experience. The personal stories are moving and well-chosen, but the authors' analyses are awkward, and the commentaries are too superficial or repetitious to be of value much of the time. Still, few books for young adults recognize the sweeping nature of the grief experience in the way this one does, and Buckingham and Huggard have marshaled a number of practical suggestions for coping as well as some excellent readings (there are some unfortunate bibliographic errors) that can supplement the material they've introduced.

Carlisle, Jock A. *Tangled Tongue: Living with a Stutterer.* 1985. Reading, Mass.: Addison-Wesley (0–201–11243–4). Ages 15–up.

Readers get a close-up of the frustrations stutterers experience in this adroit blending of personal anecdote and medical fact. Carlisle discusses causes of the disorder and various therapies used over the years to treat it, drawing on his own experiences to illuminate the everyday difficulties and the prejudices stutterers often encounter. Though Carlisle directs his text to adults, his book is accessible to teenage readers, who will find its scientific information of interest, its tone supportive, and its advice on how to go about getting help useful.

Carter, Sharon, and Lawrence Clayton. *Coping with Depression.* 1990. New York: Rosen (0–8239–1185–3). Ages 12–16.

References to music and books familiar to today's teenagers make this discussion of depression in youth more approachable than many of the young adult titles available on the subject. The authors, a free-lance writer and a family therapist who works with adolescents, keep technical terms to a minimum as they explain the difference between the "blues" and clinical depression, explore the physiological underpinnings of the illness, and pinpoint some of the environmental triggers, such as stress or a death in the family, that are thought to provoke depression. Sample case histories humanize the discussion, and the authors include simple suggestions for handling the "downers": exercise, altering the wake/sleep cycle, and eliminating

caffeine from the diet, among them. While honest about the stigma associated with therapy and emotional illness, the authors make it plain that professional intervention *can* help and urge teens to speak to an adult or seek counseling if their troubles begin to overwhelm them.

"When trouble comes, 'independence' can quickly becomes *isolation*—a sense of being stranded on an island in a dangerous sea, a sea where everyone else seems to know how to swim."
—from *Get Help*

Curtis, Robert H. *Mind and Mood: Understanding and Controlling Your Emotions.* 1986. New York: Scribner (0–684–18571–7). Ages 12–18.

Without burying readers in medical detail, Curtis explains the functioning of the nervous and endocrine systems and the link between them and human emotions. Brief definitions of familiar feelings and a look at what psychologists have discovered in the laboratory precede a fascinating discussion of nonverbal ways we communicate our moods in social situations—overtly by crying or clenching our fists, for example, or in more subtle ways, such as glancing away when we're embarrassed or feeling shy. Curtis draws on his medical background again in his exploration of how emotions can generate and aggravate disease and how various types of therapies are used to treat emotional disorders. His practical guidelines for maintaining emotional health demonstrate his faith in our ability to control at least some of what we feel.

Dinner, Sherry H. *Nothing to Be Ashamed Of: Growing Up with Mental Illness in Your Family.* 1989. New York: Lothrop (0–688–08482–6); paper (0–688–08493–1). Ages 11–15.

Dinner offers support and reassurance to young people growing up in a family altered by mental illness. Though less detailed and directed to a younger audience than Greenberg's *Emotional Illness in Your Family,* discussed elsewhere in this chapter, Dinner's text covers some of the same important territory, including discussion of symptoms and treatments for such illnesses as schizophrenia, depression, Alzheimer's disease, and anorexia. A psychologist who has worked with children, Dinner acknowledges that, while facts help, understanding and acceptance, of a condition may be difficult to achieve and that a change in family circumstances may actually be impossible. But she's convinced coping strategies are useful and discusses how readers can become more positive in their outlook and more assertive as family members, as well as where they can go to talk about their problems.

Gilbert, Sara. *Get Help.* 1989. New York: Morrow (0–688–08010–3). Ages 11–15.

Leading off with an introduction explaining how to use her directory, Gilbert presents a useful four-part catchall for young people who are dealing with a variety of growing-up concerns. Organized alphabetically by topic—abuse, addiction, adoption, through legal matters and work—the second section is the largest. It contains the addresses and phone numbers of resource agencies where immediate help or a referral can be obtained, along with some idea of the kind of help each organization offers. One unusual feature of this section is its inclusion of specific suggestions of what to say when making telephone contact, which, Gilbert explains, can be very stressful for a teenager already under emotional pressure. The last two chapters note local resources and hotline numbers. Address and phone number changes will date this book rather quickly, but with more than one hundred agencies listed, the text should still be useful for a few more years.

Greenberg, Harvey R. *Emotional Illness in Your Family: Helping Your Relative, Helping Yourself.* 1989. New York: Macmillan (0–02–736921–8). Ages 14–up.

A professor of clinical psychiatry talks about "living with other people's troubles" in a detailed book that combines medical facts with self-help guidance. To give readers a clearer understanding of various types of emotional illness, Greenberg includes a topically organized catalog of them—from anxiety-related complaints to eating disorders and illnesses that affect the elderly—explaining the symptoms and the usual medical treatment for each condition. Mindful of the dignity of the ill person as well as the needs of teenagers who live with them, he goes on to suggest age-appropriate ways young adults can assist without enabling, how they can deal with confused feelings they may have about their relative, and how they can be useful without losing perspective or becoming overwhelmed by responsibility or guilt. Filled with medical terms, the text is rather daunting and dry, but it is organized for quick reference, and it strikes at the core of what being part of a family entails.

Hyde, Margaret O., and Elizabeth Forsyth. *Horror, Fright, and Panic.* 1987. New York: Walker (0–8027–6692–7). Ages 12–15.

What is fear? Being at home alone at night? A Stephen King novel? A pop quiz at school? Hyde and Forsyth describe fear's many faces in this intriguing look at human behavior. The authors begin by defining conventional fear and looking at how it influences behavior in positive ways. They go on to examine the difference between common fear and anxiety, explain what phobias are and how they interfere with normal functioning, and discuss some of the ways modern medicine is helping people overcome extreme reactions. Widely accepted fears about death and dying, fear reactions in animals as compared with human experience, and fears born of acknowledged risks of modern technology are discussed, too, with plenty of examples to make the material colorful as well as informative. Self-help only in the broadest sense, the book deals with a subject not often popularized for teenage readers, but one that affects their lives every day.

Learning more about fear will help them cope better when they come face-to-face with the unpleasant or unknown.

Lee, Essie E., and Richard Wortman. *Down Is Not Out: Teenagers and Depression.* 1986. Englewood Cliffs, N.J.: Messner (0–671–52613–8). Ages 13–16.

Straightforward without being frightening, this accessible, authoritative overview defines the difference between the expected mood swings everyone experiences and the kind of depression that requires professional intervention. The authors, an M.D. and a professor of community health education, explain to their teenage audience how some of the normal physical and emotional changes of adolescence make young people particularly susceptible to real "downers." The authors view experiences of loss, which occur, for example, when there's death in the family or a divorce, as significant causative factors in depression and discuss them along with several other common illness triggers. Symptoms of serious illness are incorporated into the material, as are helpful summaries of recognized modern medical treatment procedures.

"It's so confusing, so difficult to explain. For the first time I see my mother as a separate person, not just as *my* mother. She's no longer the one person I can unload my daily troubles onto. She has a burden of her own." Jenny, about her mother who has cancer.

—from *Afraid to Ask*

LeShan, Eda. *When a Parent Is Very Sick.* 1986. New York: Atlantic Monthly (0–87113–095–5). Ages 11–14.

In a self-help guide for children whose parents are temporarily, chronically, or terminally ill, LeShan, a family counselor and author of many books for young people, translates keen insights about behavior into terms children can easliy understand. Punctuating her discussion with numerous anecdotes, she describes how parental behavior and family relationships alter as a result of illness in the family, explains where and how kids can get support, and deals realistically and sensitively with the confused feelings children must face in order to adjust to changes at home. She touches on a few unexpected topics as well, among them the anger that young people frequently feel after a parent's recovery. She also includes a frank chapter about death in which she urges children to become part of the mourning process. A heartfelt source of comfort that establishes the importance of expressing feelings honestly, the book can be read by a child alone or by parent and child together.

Maloney, Michael, and Rachel Kranz. *Straight Talk about Anxiety and Depression.* 1991. New York: Facts On File (0–8160–2434–0). Ages 14–18.

A responsible statement noting that "the advice and suggestions given in this book are not meant to replace professional medical and psychiatric care," prefaces this book, which is one of a handful that considers teenage stress from a real self-help perspective. Incorporating a revealing look at societal attitudes that can exacerbate anxiety-related illnesses, the authors identify common high-stress factors among teens, then clearly explain how such pressures evolve into anxiety and depression. Coping strategies suggested range from the simple and practical (exercise, read a book, clean your room) to well-detailed descriptions of sophisticated techniques such as visualization, positive self-talk, and relaxation. Biological depression is not explored, nor is there much about medication, but the authors do contribute a thoughtful discussion about the kinds of professional care that are available. Like other books in the Straight Talk series, this won't attract the audience it deserves because of its drab format.

Nida, Patricia Cooney, and Wendy
M. Heller. *The Teenager's
Survival Guide to Moving.*
1985. New York: Atheneum
(0–689–31077–3);
paper (0–02–044510–5).
Ages 12–16.

The authors chart a predictable pattern
of behavior triggered by the experience
of moving, which they identify as one of
life's most stressful events. In reasonable,
straightforward terms, they suggest how
to cope with the emotional upheaval of
leaving friends and possibly family and
offer practical suggestions for establishing
new friendships, adjusting to different
routines, and becoming involved in school
and community life. The pros and cons
of boarding with an alternate family are
described, as are some of the ways up-
rooting can affect other members of a
teenager's family—from Dad and the two-
year-old to the family pet.

VanWie, Eileen Kalberg. *Teenage
Stress.* 1987. Englewood
Cliffs, N.J.: Messner
(0–671–63824–6); paper
(0–671–65980–4).
Ages 13–16.

Make a list, take a personal inventory, keep
a journal, try deep breathing. These are but
a few of the practical suggestions tendered
in a supportive overview-workbook designed to help teenagers handle their increasingly pressured lives. Interviews with
200 junior high and high school students
helped VanWie isolate teenagers' most
common stressors, which she divides into
broad categories related to feelings about
oneself, relationships with others, and
factors such as nutrition and physical fitness. Within these groupings, she targets
specific concerns, briefly discussing such
topics as dating, handling school stress,
and communicating assertively. The book
is an accessible catchall that asks readers
plenty of insightful questions and introduces them to a helpful array of coping
strategies, most firmly rooted in common
sense.

General Health

*If You Print This, Please Don't Use
My Name.* Ed. by Nancy Keltner.
1992. Davis, Calif.: Terra Nova
Press, paper (0–944176–03–8).
Ages 13–17.

A California advice column called "FYI"
supplied the correspondence that makes
up this book, which is one of those great
items teens can pick up, put down, then
return to again and again. Arranged into
broad topical chapters, the letters (most
are from teens, though a few are from parents), signed by a variety of "Just Luckys,"
"Undecideds," and "Feeling Guilty and
Confuseds," express teens' concerns about
many burdensome physical and emotional
matters. Except for an occasional response
submitted by the FYI editor, the queries
have been answered by professionals—
physicians, psychiatrists, and other
specialists—whose credentials are supplied
in an appendix. Their responses are informal, almost conversational in tone, yet
still straight to the point. The book's graphics are amateurish, and its subject coverage
is uneven; as is usual in this type of book,
no topic is considered in much depth. But
the FYI editor wisely includes end-of-
chapter bibliographies (a mix of books for
parents and teens) that will enable readers
to investigate their concerns easily and
more fully elsewhere.

Litt, Jerome. *Teen Skin from Head
to Toe.* 1986. New York: Ballantine,
paper (0–345–32462–5).
Ages 14–18.

A practicing dermatologist since 1954, Litt
draws on his expertise to give skin, the
body's largest organ, the consideration
it deserves. His friendly tone makes the
wide-ranging text easy to read. Along with
basic skin-, hair-, and nail-care tips, he
includes some special advice on skin care
for blacks and athletes. But what distinguishes his book most from Novick's text,
following, is its top-to-toe "Anatomical
Guide to Skin Conditions," a lengthy
section that lists symptoms for everything
from acne and excess hair to lice. There's

an appropriate note that his book is not a substitute for professional care, as well as words of caution about using the over-the-counter products and procedures Litt suggests in his discussion.

Novick, Nelson Lee. *Skin Care for Teens.* 1988. New York: Watts, paper (0–531–10521–0). Ages 14–18.

Feet have a chapter of their own in this no-nonsense guide to good grooming and hygiene. Basic skin care, however, still gets most of the attention with dermatologist Novick including information on common skin problems as well as such topics as cosmetic surgery and sun damage. He also takes a look at the ingredients in a variety of soaps and cosmetics, and, like Litt, whose book was discussed previously, he recommends brand-name products (providing appropriate cautions) that he has found useful in his medical practice. Several chapters concern acne—causes, myths surrounding it, and treatments. Hair and nail care is also discussed, followed up by hygiene tips for the mouth and several other parts of the body that need special care. Though Litt's text is more medically specific, Novick's friendly tone will attract more readers.

Rosenberg, Ellen. *Growing Up Feeling Good.* 1989. Rev. ed. New York: Penguin, paper (0–14–034264–8). Ages 9–14.

A 500-page compendium now in its third revision, this book covers a lot of territory but concentrates mainly on general health. Nine- to twelve-year-olds will gravitate to the extensive section about physical maturation, which presents essential information as well as consideration of anticipated concerns. "Growing Up Feeling Good about Yourself," the second major section of the text, will attract older readers with its reflections on changing personal relationships, contraception, drugs, and family trauma. Black-and-white drawings illustrate the discussion, which Rosenberg delivers in a reassuring, non-judgmental tone.

Shaw, Diana. *Make the Most of a Good Thing: You!* 1986. New York: Atlantic Monthly Press (0–87113–039–4). Ages 11–14.

Preteen girls will find this a reassuring, positive guide that covers a variety of general health and emotional concerns. The author presents background on sexual maturation along with advice on improving physical fitness and handling the stresses that evolve from relationships with family and friends. The chapter on nutrition is particularly wide-ranging, including information on vitamin and mineral needs and advice on how to lose weight sensibly. Sexual abuse is also briefly brought up, with Shaw explaining where to go for help. The author comes out strongly against smoking and drug and alcohol use, explaining how substance abuse can compromise health during the preteen years.

Silverstein, Alvin, and Virginia B. Silverstein. *Glasses and Contact Lenses: Your Guide to Eyes, Eyewear, & Eye Care.* 1989. New York: Lippincott (0–397–32184–8). Ages 11–15.

A sprinkling of colorful anecdotes enlivens this fact-based text that will help young people gain a better understanding of how glasses and contact lenses can improve sight. Basic information on the structure and functioning of the eye prefaces an explanation of what it means to be near-sighted, farsighted, or astigmatic. Facts about corrective lenses follow, with the authors explaining what's behind those weird prescription numbers lens grinders use and examining the advantages and disadvantages of various kinds of contacts.

Silverstein, Alvin, and others. *Overcoming Acne: The How and Why of Healthy Skin Care.* 1990. New York: Morrow (0–688–08344–7). Ages 11–14.

Statistics point out that nearly 90% of young people between the ages of 12 and

17 have acne of one kind or another. That makes the subject of keen interest to teen readers. In straightforward fashion, Silverstein and his coauthors (his wife and son, in this case) examine what's known about the troublesome condition, explaining that while it cannot be cured it can be treated. As in their book *Glasses and Contact Lenses,* the authors begin with basic physiology. They then describe how acne lesions develop, what causes them, and what can be done to manage them at home (with appropriate cautions about over-the-counter products) and with the help of a dermatologist.

Simon, Nissa. *Good Sports.* 1990.
New York: HarperCollins/
Crowell (0–690–04902–1).
Ages 11–14.

Simon explains what exercise does for the body and for the mind in a helpful two-part guide that leads off with information about exercise physiology and aerobics, which she calls "the foundation for all sports." In her discussion of exercise basics she makes the importance of warm-ups and cool-downs clear and explains the kind of workout necessary to increase strength and endurance. In a section that relates nutrition to better performance, Simon suggests a simple carbohydrate diet and provides a sample menu. The book's second half focuses on sports injuries, describing some of the more common ones and explaining how factors such as steroid use or weather conditions can threaten well-being. The author stresses a sensible approach to exercise, whether a person's ultimate goal is improving physical fitness or boosting self-esteem.

Warner, Malcolm-Jamal, and Daniel
Pisner. *Theo and Me: Growing
Up Okay.* 1988. New York:
Dutton (0–525–24694–0);
NAL, paper (0–451–16216–1).
Ages 13–18.

The star who plays Theo Huxtable on NBC's popular sitcom "The Bill Cosby Show," draws on fan mail for this earnest,

wide-ranging book. One of the few such endeavors by minority writers that has been published by a mainstream press, it includes perspectives on race prejudice side-by-side with discussions about premarital sex, adjusting to a new school, and getting along with parents. Warner, the chatty voice of the text, is restrained about himself but still supplies enough personal information—about being black, being a star, and working on the Cosby show—to enliven the book. The overall result is a pleasant blend of common sense and personal opinion in which Warner makes it perfectly clear he's speaking "friend-to-friend" and his advice is no substitute for professional counsel. That's a good indication that Warner takes his responsibilities as a role model for youth very seriously.

FICTION

Bennett, James. *I Can Hear the
Mourning Dove.* 1990. New York:
Houghton (0–395–53623–5). Ages
15–18.

Sixteen-year-old Gracie, who has suffered several serious bouts of depression, wakes up in the psychiatric unit yet again. This time it takes an angry, defiant fellow patient to convince her that she's still capable of getting better and getting out.

Cooney, Caroline. *Don't Blame the
Music.* 1986. New York: Putnam
(0–448–47778–5). Ages 15–18.

Susan is happy with her life; she loves her parents and their comfortable home. But when her older sister, Ashley, comes back after touring with a rock band, Susan finds herself trying to reconcile memories of a once-caring sibling with a sister-stranger who mutilates Susan's possessions, invades her privacy, and threatens her with bodily harm.

Crutcher, Chris. *Crazy Horse Electric
Game.* 1987. New York: Greenwillow (0–688–06683–6); Dell, paper
(0–440–20094–6).
Ages 14–18.

When an injury in a water-skiing accident leaves star athlete Willie Weaver with an awkward, lurching step and slow speech, he copes by running away.

Feuer, Elizabeth. *Paper Doll.*
1990. New York: Farrar
(0–374–35736–6). Ages 15–18.

Teenager Leslie, a gifted violinist who lost her legs in a car accident, meets smart, sensitive Jeff, who has cerebral palsy. Their loving, sexual relationship helps Leslie discover courage as well as pleasure.

Getz, David. *Thin Air.* 1990. New
York: Holt (0–8050–1379–2).
Ages 11–14.

Jacob Katz suffers from crippling asthma that causes his parents to hover over him and his brother to pity him. More than anything else he wants to be in a regular sixth-grade classroom and have the kids treat him like a person who sometimes gets sick, not a person who'll never be well.

Girion, Barbara. *A Handful of Stars.*
1981. New York: Dell, paper
(0–440–93642–X). Ages 12–15.

With a wonderful part in her school play and the attentions of attractive Steve, Julie Ann couldn't be happier. Then she begins to have "spells" diagnosed as epileptic seizures, and she doesn't know how to handle the discovery.

Graber, Richard. *Doc.* 1986. New
York: Harper/Charlotte Zolotow
(0–06–022064–3). Ages 14–18.

Brad idolizes his grandfather, who used to be a respected, well-liked community doctor. But Grandpa's Alzheimer's disease is worsening, and Brad struggles with the reality that his beloved relative isn't in control anymore.

Greenberg, Joanne. *I Never
Promised You a Rose Garden.*
1964. New York: NAL, paper
(0–451–16031–2). Ages 14–up.

Committed to a mental institution when she's diagnosed as psychotic, teenager Deborah Blau describes her difficult road to recovery and the compassionate psychiatrist who helped her.

Greenberg, Joanne. *Of Such Small
Differences.* 1988. New York: Holt
(0–8050–0902–7). Ages 15–up.

Blind since birth and deaf since the age of 9, 25-year-old John Moon lives alone in a small, carefully ordered apartment, has a job, and writes poetry. When he falls in love with Leda Milan, who drives one of the vans that takes the blind to work, he feels that at last he has a chance to be part of the sighted-hearing world.

Hyland, Betty. *The Girl with the Crazy
Brother.* 1987. New York: Watts
(0–531–10345–5). Ages 12–14.

Diagnosed as schizophrenic, Dana's brilliant older brother lives at home. Though sad about his condition, she also is ashamed of him and worries that her high school friends will reject her because of the bizarre things he does. Even worse is her secret concern that she might become "crazy," too.

Jensen, Kathryn. *Pocket Change.*
1989. New York: Macmillan
(0–02–747731–2); paper
(0–590–43419–5). Ages 14–18.

Sixteen-year-old Josie Monroe is alarmed and puzzled by her beloved father's increasingly violent behavior. Unwilling to pretend nothing is amiss, she secretly investigates and concludes that her dad's experiences in Vietnam may be causing his problems now.

Klein, Norma. *Learning How to Fall.*
1989. New York: Bantam
(0–553–05809–6). Ages 15–18.

Outwardly cocky but inwardly insecure, 17-year-old Dustin Penrose has an emotional breakdown after he gets caught up in a destructive relationship with sexy, tough Star Ennis. It's Star's best friend who helps him regain his health.

Meyer, Carolyn. *Killing the Kudu.*
1990. New York: Macmillan/
Margaret K. McElderry
(0–689–50508–6).
Ages 15–18.

Helped by his cousin Scott and a beautiful
nurse, a paraplegic teenager breaks away
from his overprotective mother and finds
both love and independence.

Naylor, Phyllis Reynolds. *The
Keeper.* 1986. New York:
Atheneum (0–689–31204–0).
Ages 12–15.

Both Nick Karpinsky and his mother realize that Nick's father is mentally ill. But Mr.
Karpinsky refuses to seek help, and Nick
and his mom, powerless to force him to go
to a doctor, must cope as best they can.

O'Neal, Zibby. *Language of
Goldfish.* 1980. New York: Viking
(0–670–41785–8); Penguin, paper
(0–14–034540–X).
Ages 12–15.

Middle child in a newly affluent, happy
family, 13-year-old Carrie finds herself
less and less able to relate to her family or
make new friends at her new school. Her
unhappiness and depression deepen to the
point she no longer wants to live.

Shreve, Susan. *The Gift of the Girl
Who Couldn't Hear.* 1991.
New York: Morrow
(0–688–18318–9). Ages 11–14.

Moody and insecure, 13-year-old Eliza for-
goes a chance to sing in the class musical
only to find out that her best friend, Lucy,
who has been deaf from birth, wants to try
out. Lucy communicates orally, but she
needs Eliza to teach her how to sing.

Thiele, Colin. *Jodie's Journey.* 1990.
New York: HarperCollins
(0–06–026132–3). Ages 11–13.

Eleven-year-old Jodie is convinced that the
pain in her joints is from rigorous practice
on her beloved horse, Monarch. The
doctor, however, diagnoses rheumatoid
arthritis.

Voigt, Cynthia. *Izzy, Willy-Nilly.*
1986. New York: Atheneum
(0–689–31202–4); Fawcett, paper
(0–449–70214–6).
Ages 14–16.

When a drunk-driving accident results in
the tragic amputation of her leg, 15-year-
old Izzy Lingard struggles to accept what's
happened to her body, to her feelings, and
to her relationships with her family and
friends. The challenge makes her strong.

Sex Stuff

CONFRONTED BY BLATANT MEDIA exploitation of sex on the one hand and warnings about AIDS and pregnancy on the other, today's teens are caught in a dilemma no previous generation has had to face. If they are to make informed, active choices about their bodies and their sexual lives, they must have the facts, and with the exception of books for physically challenged teens, a wealth of material on sexuality exists. There are books meant to be shared with parents, easy-to-read paperbacks for teens whose reading skills are poor, question-answer quick-reference guides just right for browsing, and religious publications designed to reinforce particular values. Apart from religious works, which are not routinely reviewed in mainstream publications, the selections following include samples of each. The chapter begins with an interview with Lynda Madaras, who supplies some intriguing perspectives on sex education and the role of books in the learning process.

"My dad's *Playboy* magazine got me familiar with looking, and this girl in my fifth grade class got me familiar with everything else." Joe, age 16
—from *Changing Bodies, Changing Lives*

Books and Sex:
Some Perspectives from Lynda Madaras

An outspoken author of books for adults and young people, lecturer, teacher, and teen advocate, Madaras has taught sex education to students ranging in age from 9 to 18. Her popular What's Happening to My Body books about puberty (one for boys, one for girls) have each sold more than 200,000 copies and have appeared on numerous lists, including the American Library Association's Best Books for Young Adults roundup. Her latest project is entitled *The What's Happening Workbook for Girls.*

SZ: How did you come to write the What's Happening to My Body books?

LM: My daughter Area was beginning to go through some physical changes that she felt really good about. Then I saw a shift in attitude. Suddenly, she didn't want to grow up and get breasts or do any of that sort of thing. There were also changes going on in our relationship. I realized that even though Area had known details about sex from the time she was a toddler, I had not talked to her about menstruation in the same way I talked to her about other aspects of sexuality. I wanted to find a book that would communicate what I wanted to say to her. Actually, I wasn't too picky in those days. If a book didn't make sex sound like a disease and it wasn't full of hideously sexist things, it would have passed my muster. But I couldn't find one, so I wrote one.

SZ: Were you teaching while you wrote your books?

LM: What actually happened was that the head mistress of Area's school called me up and said "We have spring fever—will you come down and talk to the kids?" Of course, as soon as I walked in the classroom and said the words *penis* and *vagina* the kids just totally disintegrated. That's why I evolved the technique of coloring Xerox pictures. I talk about that in the books. I hand out pictures of the genital organs in my classes, and I have the kids color something in red, something in blue, and so on. I'm tempted every once in a while not to use pictures with the high school kids. But I've found that they allow people to do some legitimate giggling and help them deal with nervousness. I also write slang terms that kids use on the blackboard. I do that to help give kids a clearer idea of which word is appropriate in which setting—which word you can use with your mom, which you can use with the doctor, which you can use on the playground, or which might offend whom.

SZ: You gave your daughter and Dane Saavedra, the son of a neighbor, author credit. How involved in the books were they?

LM: Well, Dane just read the manuscript of the book for boys, but Area actively functioned as an editor. I'd write a chapter, and she'd read it from a kid's point of view. The books are really built up around the kinds of questions I get from kids. I think every question anyone has ever asked me is somehow covered. Of course, occasionally I'll get a new one. In the book for girls I mention one particular question from a girl who came up to me after class. She wanted to know whether a girl's breasts could burst—you know, like a balloon. It happens that developing breasts are sometimes sore, and people often make comments like "Wow, you're really busting out all over." This girl was really afraid breasts could burst. I think it's very easy for us as adults to forget how we thought about things when we were children. I'll also get deliberately lewd questions, the kind that include a lot of swear words or dirty words just to test me. But I often find these questions are sincere, too.

SZ: I suppose you learn a lot from your students.

LM: Well, I certainly get a different perspective, and I'm constantly reminded of how piecemeal the sexual information we give kids is.

SZ: Do you use your books in your classes?

LM: I follow the plan of the books, but I don't use them when I'm teaching. They are used as textbooks in a lot of schools, though. I really wrote them for parents and children to read together or to read separately and discuss. I think it's really important that parents and kids communicate about sex. When I was growing up it was the "just say no" approach. Actually, nobody even said "just say no." They never talked about sex. They wanted to protect kids from sexual experiences that might be harmful to them. But kids today are growing up in a very different world. They are bombarded by sexual messages in a way that no other generation in the history of the planet has been. We use sex to sell everything from toothpaste to dog food. The implicit message is that the goal of teen life is to have sex. Yet, teenagers get very little sexual information. What they get is usually not from their parents or from their synagogues or churches or their teachers at school. Mostly, it's from TV or from their peers, a source the kids themselves don't really trust. Obviously, the ideal situation is for parents and kids to communicate, and when parents and kids interact, having a book helps. Books make it easier for many parents to introduce the topic.

SZ: What do you feel are the hallmarks of a good sex education book for preteens?

LM: A lot of factual information about what happens to you. I get thousands of letters from kids who like the idea of the stages of development that I use in my books. For kids, having stages is like having a map—this territory has been charted. And illustrations. Kids always want to know how things work.

SZ: You integrate a lot of comments from kids into your books, don't you?

LM: Yes. I don't know if that's necessary, but it's certainly the part kids like the best. They all think they're the only ones who ever thought a particular way, so having someone else talk about the same feelings is very reassuring.

SZ: At what age should kids start reading and learning about sex?

LM: It's generally accepted in my field that if a child has gotten to be 5 and hasn't asked the "where do babies come from?" question, parents should introduce the subject. Different age groups have different interests. With toddlers, the big issue is gender identity. Adults and older children know that you're born a boy or you're born a girl and you pretty much stay that way. That's not intuitively obvious to little kids. As for older children, there's a lot of anxiety about penis size. I would say that next to the "Am I normal?" queries I get in letters, that is the major concern among boys. A boy looks at his father and looks at himself. It isn't necessarily obvious to that kid that when he grows up, his whole body grows. And it shouldn't be.

SZ: If you were to write a general sex education book for older teens who've gone through puberty, say ages 16, 17, and 18, what would you include that's different from the material you included in your books for preteens?

LM: I'd include discussion of sexual decision making. And the book should talk about love. Kids really want to know about love. I think any book for older kids would have to address feelings and emotional issues. It also has to tell kids the truth and talk about skills for saying "no" and negotiating your sexual life.

SZ: How about sexually transmitted diseases? I know you included some information on them in your books about puberty, but aren't they more of a factor for older kids?

LM: Oh, absolutely. Actually, I only added information on STDs to my puberty books with great reluctance. In the wake of the teen pregnancy epidemic and AIDS, people decided that we'd better start sex education earlier. I'm sure there's something to be said for starting prevention programs early, but too often what happens is that sex education addresses the agendas of nervous adults instead of the agendas of kids. Though it varies by community, less than 2 percent of sixth graders are sexually active. For a lot of them, a discussion of sexual decision making makes about as much sense as telling them what to pack to wear to the moon. What kids are really concerned about at that age are things like, "how come my penis curves to the left." I find that if you address kids' agendas they develop an immense gratitude. I sometimes think that if I told my kids to paint their feet blue, they would. They're just so grateful when someone tells them about all the stuff *they* are worried about. Also, if you address their concerns, they believe you care about them. Then they are more willing to listen when you talk about sexual morality or healthy rules for conducting a sexual life.

SZ: Your books are explicit. Have they had censorship problems?

LM: Yes, they've made the banned books list. Whenever a banning situation comes to my attention, I always respond personally with an open letter to the community. I've also actually gone to places and talked with the people involved. My experience has been that people get crazy and make claims that are overblown. They really hang themselves with their own rope. In every community where I've been personally involved in a banning situation, the book has been unbanned. I've also found that the vast majority of parents are really grateful for this kind of a book. I should say something here. Thank God for librarians. The Committee on Intellectual Freedom has done incredible work standing up to the book-banning mentality. I often use the fact that the American Library Association has selected the books as "best" books. Their imprimatur has meant a lot to me, not only because I'm personally honored by it but also because it carries a lot of weight in a banning situation.

NONFICTION

Puberty

Cole, Joanna. *Asking about Sex and Growing Up: A Question-and-Answer Book for Boys and Girls.* 1988. New York: Morrow (0–688–06927–4). Ages 10–13.

Although the pen-and-ink cartoon sketches (there are also several anatomical drawings) will attract mostly middle grade readers, older children will not find Cole's question-answer text patronizing in the least. In fact, its simple, forthright approach to common questions about puberty, sex, reproduction, and related matters is suitable for anyone who wants a quick, clear summary of an important part of life. Questions, printed in enlarged, boldfaced type, run the gamut from "Why do girls and women have their periods?" and "What is a wet dream?" to "Can homosexuals be parents?" and "How does a person get AIDS?" Coles also discusses pregnancy, masturbation, crushes, and birth control, delivering her information in a reassuring tone that readers will appreciate and with few value judgments.

Gardner-Loulan, JoAnn, and others. *Period.* 1991. Volcano, Calif.: Volcano Press, paper (0–912078–88–X). Ages 10–13.

Crisply drawn cartoon illustrations, generally too childlike to appeal much beyond seventh grade, depict a multicultural cast of girls celebrating femininity and the onset of menstruation. The text, originally published in 1979 and now updated to include appended guidance for parents, speaks straight to preteen readers. Including some important terminology (with pronunciation guidance), it explains menstruation in very simple terms, discusses choices available in sanitary protection (with a note about toxic shock syndrome), and deals briefly with what happens during a pelvic exam. Unfortunately, there's a cuteness about the art that cloys (a page with a uterus intended as a cutout is ludicrous), and the text is filled with generalities about emotional changes. However, kids will respond to the gentle, reassuring, almost motherly tone of the book. Later, when they're ready for a more complete picture, they can go to Madaras's excellent *What's Happening to My Body? Book for Girls* or the broader view of growing up found in McCoy and Wibblesman's *Growing & Changing*, both of which are described elsewhere in this chapter.

Glassman, Bruce. *Everything You Need to Know About Growing Up Male.* 1991. New York: Rosen (0–8239–1224–8). Ages 12–16.

While the companion book for girls in the Need to Know Library series is poorly organized and incomplete, Glassman's text for boys is a straightforward, clearly written summary that is neatly packaged into 64 easy-to-read pages and illustrated with teen-appealing photographs. Its scope is surprisingly wide; Glassman deals with facts as well as feelings related to puberty, even touching briefly on the subject of male stereotypes. Noteworthy are a chapter on personal care that discusses shaving, pimples, and mouth hygiene; an explanation of how to use condoms; and a question-answer section that supplies information about frequent teen concerns.

"I have girlfriends who think if you get into heavy petting and all that with a boy, it's stupid or artificial or something not to go all the way and have sex with him. They say sex isn't such a big deal."

—from *What's Happening to My Body? Book for Boys*

Johnson, Eric W. *Love and Sex and Growing Up.* 1990. Rev. ed. New York: Bantam (0–553–05864–9); paper (0–553–15800–7). Ages 11–13.

Though he's writing for a younger audience than he addressed in his best known book *Love and Sex in Plain Language,* described in the following section, Johnson traverses some of the same territory here, once again making clear the importance of establishing a set of personal values before making decisions about sex. Originally published in 1970, this updated edition includes information on AIDS alongside discussions of contraception, abortion, homosexuality, child sexual abuse, and heredity. Johnson also manages the amazing feat of delivering a plea for sexually responsible behavior without condescending or sounding preachy. Black-and-white captioned drawings illustrate the material, and an extensive glossary, complete with pronunciation guidelines, is appended. A multiple-choice test, which may be reproduced for school use, demonstrates Johnson's dedication to sex education in the classroom.

Johnson, Eric W. *People, Love, Sex, and Families.* 1985. New York: Walker (0–8027–6591–2). Ages 10–14.

"How do people know when they love somebody?" "Does sex feel good?" What do young people approaching puberty really want to know about sex and about love? Johnson polled 1,000 of them, ranging in age from 9 to 11, to find out. He's combined their questions and his answers into a book about sexual reproduction, love relationships, and family dynamics. Within these categories he presents information on a broad range of subjects: prejudice, homosexuality, menopause, divorce, even child abuse. Sex is clearly the main issue for many, and Johnson answers their most asked question, "How do people have babies?" in a direct, explicitly illustrated chapter that explains both intercourse and birth. A chapter on families discusses what a family is, brother-sister rivalry, and what you can do "if your parents aren't getting along very well." Material on AIDS is ready for updating, otherwise the text is a good resource for middle grade children seeking "information, please."

McCoy, Kathy, and Charles Wibbelsman. *Growing & Changing: a Handbook for Preteens.* 1987. New York: Putnam/Perigee, paper (0–399–51280–Z). Ages 11–14.

McCoy is a columnist for *Seventeen* magazine. Wibbelsman is a specialist in adolescent medicine. Together they wrote *The Teenage Body Book.* Here they target a younger audience, concentrating predominantly on the changes that come with puberty. A question-answer chapter leads off, followed by separate sections that define various stages in boys' and girls' physical development. Additional questions are scattered through remaining chapters that enlighten preteens on topics ranging from weight and nutrition to personal hygiene and emotions. There's nothing on sexually transmitted diseases such as AIDS or herpes, though some information on vaginal infections spread by other means is incorporated into a chapter about common problems of puberty. Menstrual cramps, growing pains, and scoliosis are described there, too. A friendly tone, black-and-white line drawings, and an attractive color photograph on the cover all add to the book's kid-appeal.

Madaras, Lynda, and Dane Saavedra. *The What's Happening to My Body? Book for Boys: A Growing Up Guide for Parents and Sons.* 1988. Rev. ed. New York: Newmarket (1–55704–002–8); paper (0–937858–99–4). Ages 11–15.

Boys are just as curious about what happens to their bodies during puberty as girls, but while books for girls and books for both sexes exist in plenty, not much has been written just for boys. With suggestions from 15-year-old Saavedra, the son of a friend, Madaras seeks to remedy that, providing excellent and in-depth information on all aspects of male maturation. Grounded in Madaras's experience as a California sex-education instructor, the explicit, authoritative text includes questions and comments from students in Madaras's classes as lead-ins for discussion of a variety of topics, from the stages of puberty to explanations of intercourse, birth control methods, and romantic feelings. A section on sexually transmitted diseases provides more information than is usual in books for the age group, the consideration of AIDS being particularly thorough. The book also includes information on sex-related health concerns—jock itch and testicular cancer, for example—and a chapter about puberty in girls that will answer many of the questions boys have about the opposite sex. While the main text is addressed to young readers, the introduction is for parents, whom Madaras urges to become involved in their children's sexual education.

Madaras, Lynda, and Area Madaras. *The What's Happening to My Body? Book for Girls: A Growing Up Guide for Parents and Daughters.* 1988. Rev. ed. New York: Newmarket (1–55704–001–X); paper (0–937858–98–6). Ages 11–15.

As in her book for boys, just described, Madaras combines puberty and sex education information in one frank, comprehensive volume for preteens, early adolescents, and parents. Writing as much from her vantage point as a woman and mother of a girl (her daughter Area helped inspire her) as from her experience as a school sex-educator, Madaras presents a complete review of changes accompanying puberty in girls, devoting separate chapters to breasts, changes in the genital and reproductive organs, and the menstrual cycle. With a few changes relevant to gender, subsequent chapters on sexual health, intimacy and birth control, and love are virtually identical to her discussions in the boys' book. Drawings are also included, as is a chapter summarizing pubertal change in the opposite sex.

Marzollo, Jean. *Getting Your Period.* 1989. New York: Dial (0–8037–0355–4); paper (0–8037–0356–2). Ages 11–15.

Marzollo takes some of the mystery out of puberty in a reassuring book that makes it plain "there is no perfectly 'normal' way to have your period. Instead there are lots of normal ways. . . ." Using a combination of straightforward description and commonly asked questions, she explains just a bit about what happens to the body during puberty before focusing on what to expect when menstruation begins. She includes illustrated, well-detailed information about different types of sanitary protection as well as common-sense advice about accepting menstruation as a part of life and managing the practical difficulties it entails. Though the book's main audience will be 11- and 12-year-olds, its sophisticated cover and unpatronizing tone will make it attractive even to older junior high girls who've yet to get their periods.

Nourse, Alan E. *Menstruation.*
1987. New York: Watts
(0–531–10308–0).
Ages 11–15.

There's none of the reassuring tone of Marzollo's book in this one, but there is a lot of information, lucidly presented and nicely illustrated. Nourse is best at conveying medical specifics, and he provides readers with an excellent summary of what happens during menstruation. His discussions of toxic shock and premenstrual syndromes are also good, including information on toxic shock symptoms and causes and a review of the great debate surrounding PMS—does it really exist? Concluding that it does, he supplies common-sense guidelines to help young women recognize and cope with some of its manifestations.

Packer, Kenneth. *Puberty: The
Story of Growth and Change.*
1989. New York: Watts
(0–531–10810–4).
Ages 11–14.

The textbookish dust jacket on this book isn't the least bit inviting, but the nicely executed, clearly labeled drawings inside will help keep readers interested in what Packer has to say about puberty. Like Nourse, Packer concentrates on physiology, not feelings. In straightforward fashion he summarizes what happens during the growth spurt, introduces the male and female reproductive systems, and outlines the processes of conception and birth. A few health and hygiene issues come under discussion—toxic shock syndrome, testicular and breast cancer, among them—but nothing is said about sexually transmitted diseases. Nor is there much on contraception, a subject of great importance even to the preteen audience Packer addresses. What is actually presented is clear and well-organized, though. For a more inclusive view of the subject, readers can turn to *Changing Bodies, Changing Lives,* listed in the following section, or either of Lynda Madaras's preteen books, all three of which Packer wisely suggests in his bibliography.

Rench, Janice E. *Teen Sexuality.*
1988. Minneapolis: Lerner
(0–8225–0041–8). Ages 12–15.

Rench packs a lot into this 72-page book that defines sexuality as a mix of feelings, physical responses, and interpersonal relationships. Fictional profiles of teenagers head chapters that consider each of these components and present frank, thoughtful answers to common questions: "What choices do I have when I'm feeling pressured by my boyfriend?" "What does sexual intercourse feel like?" Not only filled with facts, the responses also promote a better understanding of the consequences of certain behaviors. In answer to a question about pornography, for example, Rench writes "it can be wrong to look at pornography if your attitudes about the opposite sex are being formed by what you see." While she urges teenagers to take responsibility for their own sexual health, she includes only brief information on sexually transmitted disease. Boys may pick up this book, though it speaks louder to girls, and with enlarged type and concise text gathered under boldfaced headings, it will particularly appeal to reluctant readers. Rench's bibliography contains some excellent follow-up titles (among them Madaras's books, listed previously) that can satisfy a teenager's desire for more details.

Beyond Basics

Bell, Ruth, and others. *Changing
Bodies, Changing Lives.*
1988. Rev. ed. New York:
Random (0–394–56499–5);
paper (0–394–75541–3).
Ages 14–18.

Published first in 1981 and now out in the second edition, this is one of the best and most comprehensive books for young people who need information on their physical and emotional maturation. Bringing together material for both sexes, it addresses a wide range of concerns, answering questions about everything from menstruation and what people do during sex to getting along with parents, handling depression, being gay, and undergoing a medical checkup. The authors are generally nonjudgmental in their discussion of sexual activity among teens, though they caution readers against casual sex and include information on AIDS in their section on sexually transmitted diseases. They also demonstrate concern over teenage drinking and driving. Embarrassed teens can't tuck this oversized book into their pocket or purse, but the colorful photo-collage on the cover will attract readers anyway, as will the black-and-white photographs used inside, which capture real emotions on the faces of real kids. First-person comments humanize the discussion and add an element of shared experience to this impressive portrait of growing up.

Booher, Dianna Daniels. *Love.* 1985.
　　Englewood Cliffs, N.J.: Messner
　　(0–671–54401–2). Ages 12–16.

"Am I in love?" "Is there really such a thing as 'love at first sight?'" "Can I love two people at the same time?" Aiming her discussion at teenage girls, Booher answers these and other commonly asked questions, challenging kids to look closely at their relationships and be honest about what they find. She does a good job of explaining the kinds of things that distinguish a mature relationship, including where physical attractiveness and personality fit in. Misconceptions about love, exploitive attachments, and breaking up are also discussed. Booher concludes that while sexual intimacy won't always be part of teenagers' loving relationships, it often is, and she devotes a chapter to "the difference between having sex and making love."

Boston Children's Hospital. *What
　　Teenagers Want to Know About
　　Sex: Questions and Answers.*
　　1988. Boston: Little, Brown
　　(0–316–25063–5). Ages 14–18.

The delivery is dry and answers are rarely more than a paragraph or two, yet this frank question-answer book is loaded with specifics on all sorts of sex-related issues. Topically organized, the queries range widely: "What does *gang bang* mean?" "Are orgasms emotional or physical or both?" "Is it OK to exercise during menstruation?" Many common concerns are addressed, but a few unusual sections stand out. The book's last chapter, for example, is devoted to questions about infertility, an unusual topic for a teenage sex-information book. All answers have behind them the authority of the chief of the Division of Adolescent and Young Adult Medicine at Boston Children's Hospital. An excellent glossary and helpful illustrations round out the presentation, which is tailor-made for readers who want the facts in small chunks for quick reference.

Johanson, Sue. *Talk Sex.* 1989.
　　New York: Penguin, paper
　　(0–14–010377–5). Ages 14–18.

Involved in the field of sex education since 1972, Johanson is a registered nurse and host of "Talking Sex with Sue," a Canadian radio show aimed at teenagers. *Talk Sex* is based on questions she has discovered in the "Dear Sue" boxes she places in the schools she visits as a lecturer. The subjects they deal with are complex and important, from body image, love, romance, and sexual identity to prostitution and sexual abuse. Johanson's answers are forthright and explicit, but her coverage is uneven. Birth control, for example, receives only brief attention, while masturbation and orgasm are discussed much more frankly and in greater detail than is usual in books for teenagers. In fact there's a whole chapter on what Johanson calls "the big O." Other examples of flip phraseology ("Get your buns in to the doctor," "Go for the burn") leap out elsewhere, though it's not likely that kind of pretentiousness will stop teens from skimming the text. That the author regularly encourages readers to seek more information from a trained health professional is a good indication of her concern for teens. Unfortunately there is no index.

Johnson, Eric W. *Love and Sex
　　in Plain Language.* 1988.
　　Rev. ed. New York: Bantam
　　(0–553–27473–2); paper
　　(0–553–25400–6). Ages 14–18.

Now in its fourth edition, Johnson's astute overview of love and sex clarifies the responsibilities involved in becoming sexually active. Along with subjects commonly covered—sexual anatomy, birth control, sexually transmitted diseases, and so forth—come discussions of matters less routine, for example, the ways popular songs, TV, and movies influence sexual attitudes. When reviewing contraception, Johnson includes more information on natural family planning than is usual in this kind of book (though he does not recommend the method for young adults), and his detailed description of a newborn may startle teenagers who think babies are always cute and quiet. Johnson writes with appealing informality, avoiding text-book jargon while still managing to be explicit. But what really makes the book stand out is Johnson's quietly but firmly stated conviction that sexual intimacy must be rooted in real caring and carefully considered personal values. There's an excellent glossary as well as a mastery test that can be reproduced for school use.

McCoy, Kathy, and Charles Wibbelsman. *The New Teenage Body Book*. 1992. New York: Putnam/Perigee, paper (0–399–51725–X). Ages 14–18.

Frank questions make effective, informal lead-ins to the high interest discussion topics included in this wide-ranging book about adolescence. Writing both to young men and young women, the authors combine responsive counsel, common sense instruction, and facts about many physical and emotional matters—nutrition, pregnancy, parenthood, homosexuality, physical and emotional development. Queries run the gamut from ''How do you make love?'' and ''Will I be a virgin if I use tampons?'' to ''Is it selfish to say 'No' to sex?'' and ''How old do you have to be to worry about cholesterol?'' The authors come out strongly against the use of alcohol, tobacco, and recreational drugs, and take a cautionary view of premarital sex, acknowledging that the decision to become physically intimate is a highly personal one. For teens who choose to become involved, they include solid information on contraception, sexually transmitted diseases,

and guidelines for safer sex practices. Though a bit more strident in tone than *Changing Bodies,* listed previously, this book has more recent information on STDs and birth control, including descriptions of the Norplant system and vaginal contraceptive film. Illustrations are scattered through the text.

Nourse, Alan E. *Birth Control*. 1988. New York: Watts (0–531–10516–4). Ages 12–18.

Though its closely packed type and unattractive dust jacket will put off a lot of readers, this book is a thorough, clear-cut study of a subject of great importance even to preteens. With medical terminology appearing in boldface, the author spells out the pros and cons of most of the currently accepted contraceptive methods (the newer contraceptive implant is not discussed). Abortion *is* included in the birth control inventory, with an explanation that, while it is not actually a contraceptive, it is a ''last resort method of birth control,'' which is, ''right or wrong . . . a fact in the world today.'' The author's style is dry, but he provides a wealth of information. His description of the rhythm method, for example, is much more than the usual paragraph or two. And when he talks about contraceptive pills, he makes certain readers understand that more than one kind exists. Nourse, a physician, is a prolific, reliable author of medical information books for young people. It's too bad this one won't attract more readers.

Nourse, Alan E. *Teen Guide to Birth Control*. 1988. New York: Watts (0–531–10625–X). Ages 12–16.

Teenagers reluctant to pick up Nourse's comprehensive *Birth Control,* described previously, might be willing to browse through this nicely illustrated abbreviated version. It's a respectable distillation of the full-length book, with numerous color photographs, drawings, and a crisp, uncrowded format. Nourse is, as usual, sincere, straightforward, and even-handed. This book is part of the Teen Guide series of high-interest, easy-to-read books, as is the following book.

Nourse, Alan E. *Teen Guide to
Safe Sex.* 1988. New York:
Watts (0–531–10592–X).
Ages 12–16.

Writing in his characteristically earnest
voice, Nourse provides young people with
direct, accessible information on sexually
transmitted diseases. He identifies eleven
of the most common ones, including AIDS,
and explains briefly what they are and what
their symptoms and complications may be.
He then furnishes suggestions for safer sex
practices, including detailed instructions
for using condoms. Though he states outright that he hopes teens will postpone
sexual intimacy "at least for the time
being," he doesn't lecture. Colorful, well-
chosen photographs brighten the concise,
down-to-earth text.

Voss, Jacqueline, and Jay Gale.
*A Young Woman's Guide to
Sex.* 1986. Los Angeles: Price
Stern, paper (0–89586–692–7).
Ages 14–up.

Here's another book with a drab cover
and a dense-looking format, but young
women seriously interested in learning
about their bodies will find it full of valuable information. A clinical psychologist and
sex educator, Voss is the matter-of-fact
voice of the coauthored book that deals,
often explicitly, with emotional and physical concerns. Along with discussion of
expected topics, such as puberty, birth
control, pregnancy, and STDs, comes
information on the male body, sexual
dysfunction, and sexual decision making.
One particularly unusual section describes
what a first sexual experience might be like.
There's also a nicely done chapter on
sexual identity, though it refers to a follow-
up resource (*A Way of Life, A Way of Love:
A Young Person's Introduction to What
It Means to Be Gay* by Hanckel and
Cunningham) that is now out of date in
several important respects. Despite that,
this is still a respectable overview that
can take over where Madaras's book for
younger girls stops. A useful list of resource
agencies and an excellent glossary conclude
the book.

Being Gay

Cohen, Susan, and Daniel Cohen.
*When Someone You Know
Is Gay.* 1989. New York:
Evans (0–87131–567–X).
Ages 14–18.

The experiences and comments of teenagers supply a compelling human element
here, but the Cohens' informally voiced,
broad-minded perspectives are just as
pivotal to this frank look at gay and lesbian
life. Included is information about coming
out, sex, homosexual parenting, and how
AIDS has affected the gay community,
along with highlights of gay history "from
Plato to Stonewall," and a controversial
chapter, incorporating biblical references,
that investigates how mainstream religions
view homosexuals today. The authors address typical misconceptions in an early
section presented in question-answer form:
"Is it a sin?" "Do gay men hate women?"
"If I'm the friend of somebody who's
gay, won't they think I'm gay too?" A
later chapter features lengthy, candid interviews with a drag queen, a transvestite,
and a transsexual, which clarify different
behaviors that are often confused. The
authors address their text to nongays who
seek a better understanding of a different

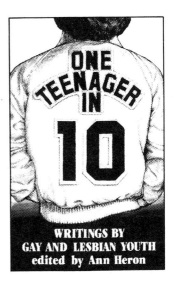

way of life, but they also supply much of value to teenagers struggling with their sexual identity.

One Teenager in Ten: Writings by Gay and Lesbian Youth. Ed. by Ann Heron. 1983. Boston: Alyson, paper (0–932870–26–0). Ages 14–up.

Accounts from 27 young men and women who have acknowledged their homosexuality, at least to themselves, personalize familiar statistics that count one out of every ten teenagers as gay. Ranging in age from 15 to 24, the young people, most from the United States, reflect big-city and small-town values as they speak articulately about discovering their sexuality. One or two speak explicitly about their first sexual encounter, but sexual behavior is not what they discuss most. Nor is sexual health a priority concern. Instead, the young people concentrate on emotional issues—in particular their experiences coming out to parents and friends and their difficulties establishing contact with a gay support community. Though their testimonies are sometimes bleak, more often than not they reverberate with hope. By and large these are profiles of strong kids who've successfully found their own way.

"It was okay to be gay, okay to be different. And being different didn't mean a life of loneliness and solitude. I learned that my friends and I could be different together. I was not merely out of the closet, I was out of the coffin." Aaron Fricke
—from *One Teenager in Ten*

Rench, Janice E. *Understanding Sexual Identity: A Book for Gay Teens and Their Friends.* 1990. Minneapolis: Lerner (0–8225–0044–2). Ages 12–15.

Rench provides reassurance as she reaches out to teenagers who know they are gay

or simply want some general information on the subject. Fictional scenarios head the chapters, which are presented in question-answer form. Topics range widely—from homophobia and AIDS to gay parents and religious attitudes toward homosexuality. Though concise and forthright most of the time, Rench's answers are occasionally evasive or oversimplified. For example, to the question "What do gay couples do together?" Rench responds ". . . all human beings do a variation of the same things for and to each other in a sexual relationship." Readers who want more complete answers can turn to *When Someone You Know Is Gay* or *Changing Bodies, Changing Lives,* both of which Rench has included in her helpful bibliography. Like the author's book *Teen Sexuality,* listed previously, this is a slim book, more simply written than most materials on the subject.

Sexually Transmitted Diseases

Blake, Jeanne. *Risky Times: How to Be AIDS-Smart and Stay Healthy.* 1990. New York: Workman, paper (0–89480–655–4). Ages 14–18.

A Massachusetts-based medical reporter focuses on risky behaviors, not risk groups, in this compassionate, eye-catching paperback designed to present sexually active teenagers with information about AIDS. Concentrating on transmission factors, treatment and testing, and the use of condoms, Blake delivers information in clear, no-nonsense terms young adults will understand as well as appreciate. However, it's the plainspoken words of other individuals whom Blake gathered together—concerned young adults, AIDS sufferers, and celebrities such as Martin Short, Cher, and Matthew Broderick—that go furthest toward convincing teenagers to "stop thinking they are immortal and start thinking about being safe." Black-and-white photographs individualize the speakers and give the text browser appeal. A free parent's guide, written by teen advice columnist Beth Winship, is being distributed concurrently.

Colman, Warren. *Understanding and Preventing AIDS.* 1988. Chicago: Childrens Press (0–516–00592–8). Ages 11–15.

Though the story of teenage AIDS sufferer Ryan White, with which Colman begins, now needs a postscript—Ryan died in 1991—this book is still in several ways a useful resource. With excellent photographs and diagrams backing up the explanations, Colman tells how the HIV virus does its damage. Without being graphic, he details how AIDS is spread, then goes on to answer commonly asked questions and alert readers to important guidelines for preventing infection. Colman's stand against teen sex and drug use will make the book popular among parents. With good AIDS material for middle-graders in short supply, this should be a useful book, although the book is more classroom text than self-help guidebook.

Daugirdas, J.T. *STD: Sexually Transmitted Diseases.* 2d ed. 1991. Hinsdale, Ill.: MedText, Inc. (0–9629279–0–2). Ages 14–18.

This fact-filled text focuses on six of the most common sexually transmitted diseases, among them AIDS and syphilis. Sophisticated cartoon drawings add enough humor to make the information go down easily, but there's no attempt to personalize and no soft soaping when it comes to the facts. Information about symptoms and testing procedures is particularly specific, and Daugirdas includes an excellent section explaining the importance of partner notification, a topic often glossed over in sex-education materials. Diagrams depicting illness symptoms (geometrical representations of sexual anatomy with lightning bolts and tear drops indicating pain and discharge) are too absurd to be of any help to readers. Teens will also see right through the three "case reports" that round out the text: they're little more than undisguised lessons about the unanticipated consequences of risky sexual behavior. For a closer look at AIDS and its effects, teens can turn to Blake's *Risky Time* or *Lynda Madaras Talks to Teens about AIDS,* but single volumes as comprehensive as those books don't exist for young adults on the other major STDs. Despite its drawbacks, Daugirdas's overview will help fill that information gap. Drawings aside, it's a solid, no-nonsense, quick-reference source, that has recently been adopted for use by the Chicago Public School System Department of Science.

Madaras, Lynda. *Lynda Madaras Talks to Teens about AIDS: An Essential Guide for Parents, Teachers, and Young People.* 1988. New York: Newmarket, (1–55704–010–9); paper (1–55704–009–5). Ages 14–18.

Readers won't find much about the discovery, symptoms, or treatment of AIDS here. Instead, Madaras concentrates on risky behaviors and the ways people can protect themselves from contracting the virus. Though she acknowledges that sex is going to be part of many teens' lives, Madaras is really an advocate of sexual abstinence for teenagers. To help kids deal with sexual pressure without the threat of HIV exposure, she suggests alternatives to intercourse that allow intimacy without compromising safety and offers advice on how to stick to a decision to remain celibate. For young adults who *are* sexually active, she presents a thorough discussion of condoms, including illustrated instructions for their use. Her information on intravenous drug transmission is equally detailed, with diagrammed instructions on how to sterilize needles with bleach. Madaras is authoritative and explicit here; she also demonstrates great concern for the young. A foreword for parents and teachers encourages them to become part of the AIDS education process.

Nourse, Alan E. *Teen Guide to AIDS Prevention.* 1990. New York: Watts (0–531–10966–6). Ages 12–15.

A companion to Nourse's *Teen Guide to Safe Sex,* written for reluctant readers, this easy-to-read book is a well-organized summary of AIDS facts presented in an attractive format that will draw a large readership. Nourse concentrates mostly on medical aspects of the virus; there's little about the social ramifications. But he includes a chapter, "Staying Free of HIV," that explains basic ways to protect oneself. Well-chosen, full-color photographs scattered through the text are good inducements to browsers.

FICTION

Blume, Judy. *Are You There, God? It's Me Margaret.* 1970. New York: Bradbury (0–02–710990–9); Dell, paper (0–440–40419–3). Ages 11–14.

When 12-year-old Margaret worries, she talks to God. It seems she's been worrying a lot lately—about her family, about people she knows, and about getting her first period.

Byars, Betsy. *The Burning Questions of Bingo Brown.* 1988. New York: Penguin, paper (0–14–032479–8). Ages 11–14.

Though sixth-grader Bingo Brown isn't sure what love actually is, he is certain he "fell in love three times during English class."

Garden, Nancy. *Annie on My Mind.* 1982. New York: Farrar (0–399–21046–6); paper (0–374–40413–5). Ages 15–18.

High school students Annie and Liza meet at New York City's Metropolitan Museum of Art. It isn't long before they discover they're falling in love.

Hamilton, Virginia. *A Little Love.* 1984. New York: Putnam (0–399–21046–6). Ages 15–18.

Sheema feels slow and fat and insecure, even though her boyfriend Forrest loves her and finds her desirable. It takes a trip with Forrest to find the father who left her at birth to complete her rites of passage.

Homes, A. M. *Jack.* 1989. New York: Macmillan (0–02–744831–2). Ages 14–18.

After Jack's father reveals he is gay, the puzzling aspects of Jack's parents' acrimonious divorce suddenly fall into place.

Klein, Norma. *Just Friends.* 1990. New York: Knopf (0–679–80213–4). Ages 15–18.

Though Isabel doesn't realize it at first, she's in love with Stuart, who's been her New York City neighbor and friend since they were both small. When Stuart has an affair with Iz's pretty friend, jealous Isabel decides it's time she has her first sexual experience.

Klein, Norma. *My Life as a Body.* 1987. New York: Knopf (0–394–89051–5); Fawcett, paper (0–449–70265–0). Ages 15–18.

Intelligent but insecure, 17-year-old Augie is troubled by her sexual inexperience. When she agrees to tutor disabled classmate Sam, she has no idea she will fall in love with him or that their relationship will help her discover how to balance her physical and intellectual needs.

Koertge, Ron. *The Arizona Kid.*
1988. Boston: Little, Brown
(0–316–50101–8); Avon,
paper (0–380–70776–4).
Ages 15–18.

Insecure, height-conscious Billy doesn't
know what to expect when he arrives in
Arizona for the summer. For the most part,
he's pleased with what he finds: his gay
uncle Wes is funny and caring; he likes his
coworker Lew; and he has his first sexual
experience with pretty Cara Mae.

Mazer, Norma Fox. *Up in Seth's
Room.* 1979. New York: Dell,
paper (0–440–99190–0).
Ages 16–18.

Finn is certain she loves handsome 19-year-
old Seth and that he loves her. But she's
also sure she wants to remain a virgin for
the time being.

Miklowitz, Gloria. *Good-bye
Tomorrow.* 1987. New York:
Delacorte (0–385–29562–6); Dell,
paper (0–440–20081–4).
Ages 14–16.

When a blood transfusion leaves popular
high school senior Alex with ARC (AIDS
Related Complex) and the news leaks out,
some of his classmates shun him; others
rally to his side.

Vail, Rachel. *Wonder.* 1991. New
York: Watts/Orchard/Richard
Jackson (0–531–05964–2).
Ages 11–14.

Taunted by girls who used to be her
friends (they dub her Wonder on the first
day of school because her dress looks
like a Wonder bread wrapper), and uncomfortable with her new adolescent body,
seventh-grader Jessica salvages her pride
by pretending not to care. Then along
comes Conor O'Malley, who becomes her
first boyfriend.

One Plus One Makes Three

MORE THAN ONE MILLION teenage girls become pregnant each year, but though a lot of adult books on parenting and pregnancy exist, only recently have we begun to see books that deal specifically with young parents' or pregnant teenagers' particular health, economic, and emotional concerns. These materials, many of which ignore fathers, often lack the finesse of adult books: their graphics are usually dull, their texts prosaic, and their organization imprecise. For these reasons, this chapter includes titles published for adults as well as some of the best of the books meant for teens.

"Last semester I got pregnant and I would sit in bed at night, every night, and say, 'I don't believe this, this can't be happening to me. Go away. Leave me alone. I can't handle this.'" Bev, age 16

—from *Changing Bodies, Changing Lives*

NONFICTION

Marriage

Ayer, Eleanor H. *Everything You Need to Know About Teen Marriage.* 1990. New York: Rosen (0-8239-1221-3). Ages 12–16.

Like Glassner's *Growing Up Male,* listed in a previous section, this book is part of the Need to Know Library series directed to reluctant readers. It uses a modified question-answer approach, shot through with the comments of young adults, to present a simplified view of what marriage involves—dirty socks and diapers as well as passion, trust, and caring. Ayer sees marriage as a risky proposition, and she weights her words accordingly ("When you have an argument with your date, isn't it nice to go home?"). But she isn't overtly preachy, and she does not ignore the fact that some teen marriages do work. She includes the remarks of teens who are happily married right alongside the words of those who've found getting hitched was a big mistake. Appealing color photographs featuring teens will attract browsers as will the book's spacious format. While Ayer falls a good deal short of discussing "everything you need to know," she does introduce quite a lot in under 100 pages.

Lindsay, Jeanne Warren. *Teenage Marriage: Coping with Reality.* 1988. Rev. ed. Buena Park, Calif.: Morning Glory Press (0-930934-31-8); paper (0-930934-30-X). Ages 12–18.

Emphasizing that it takes effort on the part of *both* partners to make a marriage work, Lindsay explores the particular problems young married couples face in a book originally published in 1981. Comments from experts and remarks from teenagers combine in a overview that touches lightly on everything from what it's like living with in-laws and being broke to the effect children have on marital relationships. This is a book with a message that's sure to make make teenagers think twice before they march down the aisle.

Lindsay, Jeanne Warren. *Teens Look at Marriage: Rainbows, Roles, and Realities.* 1985. Buena Park, Calif.: Morning Glory Press (0-930934-16-4); paper (0-930934-15-6). Ages 12–18.

The responses of three thousand teenagers, most unmarried, who participated in a survey conducted by Lindsay form the nucleus of this revealing book. The author's questionnaire, which appears at the back of the book, prompted teens to consider everything from who might discipline the children to the ways in which ethnic or religious differences might affect marital relationships. Graphs accompany a summary of Lindsay's findings, which she's fortified with comments teens wrote on their papers and responses she collected during personal interviews. Teenagers contemplating marriage will find the book filled with interesting insights, even though its format is less suited to independent reading than to classroom use.

Pregnancy

Bowe-Gutman, Sonia. *Teen Pregnancy.* 1987. Minneapolis: Lerner (0-8225-0039-6). Ages 12–16.

Though the dust jacket looks more like it belongs on a dreamy teenage novel than on a book of nonfiction, there's nothing soft-edged about the information inside this book. Bowe-Gutman, who debunks the idea that having sex is part of a teenager's rite of passage, urges young people to consider their personal values and their parenting readiness carefully before embarking on a sexual relationship of any kind. Though not overtly judgmental of young people who are having sex, her discussion sounds very much like a lecture at times, with information on health risks for teen mothers and babies, child-care costs, and profiles of pregnant teens that are really little more than thinly disguised roundups of the problems pregnant teens need to face. Still, the issues she raises are vital ones, and that plus clear, well-illustrated chapters on conception and contraception make her simplified approach of value, especially to young teens and older ones whose reading skills are insufficient to enable them to handle more complicated discussions.

Brown, Fern G. *Teen Guide to Caring for Your Unborn Baby.* 1989. New York: Watts (0–531–10668–3). Ages 12–16.

Diagrams and excellent photographs, many picturing teenage mothers-to-be, add browser appeal to this primer on prenatal care and pregnancy. Simplified to suit the information needs of readers unwilling or unable to handle more complete materials about pregnancy, it is a practical, useful guide that touches on prenatal-care concerns ranging from nutrition, exercise, and what to expect during each trimester of development to common complaints such as nausea and backaches. Important terms in boldfaced type within the text are included in a glossary. The book is part of the same high-interest, easy-to-read series as Brown's book on childbirth, following, and Nourse's book *Birth Control,* reviewed in the previous chapter.

Brown, Fern G. *Teen Guide to Childbirth.* 1988. New York: Watts (0–531–10573–3). Ages 12–16.

Part of the Teen Guide series, this book is filled with full-color photos and diagrams that make it every bit as visually interesting as Brown's parenting primer, *Teen Guide to Caring For Your Unborn Baby.* Here, Brown deals with the culmination of pregnancy, divesting it of some of its mystery by simply and clearly presenting basic facts. Working in comments from three sets of expectant teenage parents, she describes different birth settings and health care providers (doctors, nurses, midwives), introduces a few of the more familiar birth methods, and explains labor and delivery, from Braxton Hicks contractions and cesarean section to Apgar scores and postpartum depression. Curious teens as well as parents-to-be will find the text encouraging and forthright.

"When you think you might be pregnant it's one thing. When someone tells you your test is positive, that's a whole new ball game." Arlene
—from *What Do I Do Now?*

Ewy, Donna, and Roger Ewy. *Teen Pregnancy: The Challenges We Faced; The Choices We Made.* 1984. Boulder, Colo.: Pruett Publishing, paper (0–87108–652–2). Ages 12–18.

The 1984 publication date means the authors' section on birth control is out-of-date (there's no mention of the contraceptive sponge, for example, let alone the long lasting subdermal birth control implant), but this is still a book with great appeal for teenage girls. Filled with charts, several types of sketches, and black-and-white photographs of young women involved in a Colorado pregnant-teens program, it is as eye-catching as it is eye-opening. It begins with a photo-text scrapbook of personal profiles. Young women between the ages of 13 and 19 introduce themselves and briefly describe their circumstances. Successive chapters present information on conception and fetal development, the physical and emotional changes mothers-to-be experience, nutrition and exercise, signs that something's amiss, and the birth process itself. Particularly noteworthy is a discussion of the importance of a support system for pregnant teens. Common questions about these topics head each chapter. Reprinted in enlarged type in the chapter itself, the questions are answered in largely nontechnical terms. The book points out many obstacles facing teenage mothers, but its outlook is not overwhelmingly bleak. "Teen pregnancy may be full of challenges," the authors write, "but it doesn't mean that all is lost." A final chapter makes good use of the experiences of young women in the Colorado program: they comment openly on different types of birth control and counsel "our teen sisters" on when, why, and how to say "no" to having sex. Photos are uneven in quality and the book contains some fill-the-blank sections libraries probably won't like, but the artless, plainspoken testimonies of girls who've "been there" still compel attention and are more browsable and easier to read than the ones in Kuklin's *What Do I Do Now?*, listed later in this chapter.

Kitzinger, Sheila. *Being Born.* 1986.
    Photographs by Lennart Nilsson.
    New York: Grosset
    (0–448–18990–9). Ages 11–up.

Extraordinary full-color intrauterine photographs taken by a renowned medical photographer are the touchstone of this 64-page book that provides a glimpse of the miracle of prenatal development. Set against dramatic black backgrounds, the photographs follow the progression of the fetus from conception through birth. Kitzinger's text, written as though readers are experiencing their own prenatal metamorphosis, is a lyrical description of each developmental stage: "Once you were in a small, dark place inside your mother's body . . . you didn't look much like a baby yet—more like a sprouting bean . . . then, like a tiny seahorse, you grew little ridges down your back. . . ." A touching photograph of first bonding, a picture of the newborn infant at its mother's breast, is a marvelous finale. The book is a beautifully designed, sensitive celebration of new life that speaks to readers of many ages about a common journey.

Kitzinger, Sheila. *The Complete Book of Pregnancy and Childbirth.*
    Rev. ed. 1989. New York:
    Knopf (0–394–58011–7).
    Ages 14–up.

The author of sixteen previous books on pregnancy, parenting, and related subjects (see *Being Born,* previous citation), Kitzinger brings her expertise to bear in this comprehensive manual, which begins with an impressive color-photo birth sequence. Published for adults (adults appear in the photos), the book deals with some issues teens won't have encountered as yet.

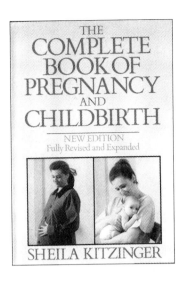

What's more, Kitzinger doesn't consider specific problems teen parents face, as do Lindsay and Brunelli in their prenatal care guidebook, *Teens Parenting: Your Pregnancy and Newborn Journey.* What makes Kitzinger's text of value to young adults is her extraordinarily clear explanation of developing life, information important to expectant mothers of all ages. A strong sense of Kitzinger's respect for that life fills the pages as she describes the physical and emotional changes to mother and baby that occur during pregnancy, from pregnancy confirmation to the first hours after birth. She even includes a chapter especially for expectant fathers and another that discusses the anguish of miscarriage, a tragedy that does affect pregnant teens. With its lucid, well-organized text, arresting photos, and helpful drawings, the book is an excellent resource.

Kuklin, Susan. *What Do I Do Now?:
    Talking about Teenage
    Pregnancy.* 1991. New York:
    Putnam (0–399–21843–2);
    paper (0–399–22043–7).
    Ages 13–18.

Filled with sharp details about the girls and their circumstances, Kuklin's gritty book presents a close-up view of what it's like to be a pregnant teenager today. The author, who selected interviewees from among people who visited several New

York area agencies (a Planned Parenthood affiliate, a clinic licensed to perform abortions, and an adoption agency), followed more than a dozen girls from different racial and economic backgrounds into their homes, into their counseling sessions, and even into examining rooms. Merging their personal comments and perspectives from health professionals and parents with her

own research, Kuklin has produced an affecting collective portrait. Some situations will shock readers: a mother who gives up her bedroom to her daughter and the girl's boyfriend; a girl who threatens the father of her baby with a butcher knife. But Kuklin does not judge. Neither does she overtly politicize, though political issues are raised by some of the people she spoke with. For example, she includes comments from members of an abortion clinic staff who talk about right-to-life pickets protesting outside. Kuklin's viewpoint is an urban one; the small town girl's dilemma isn't really addressed here. Nor is there much about birth control methods, though the situations described present convincing evidence of the need for better birth control education. Teenage fathers contribute a few perspectives but are, by and large, not heard from enough. Yet what *is* here is unforgettable, and it's more than enough to cause at least some teens to think twice before putting themselves at risk for parent-

hood. A more rigorous and demanding book than the Ewys' book described in a previous citation.

"Boy! Am I in a trap. I'll just have to take it one day at a time until the baby's born. I swear that I will be there for the baby, my son. But Jackie is another story. I'm trying my best, but I'm not going to push a bad thing." George
—from *What Do I Do Now?*

Lindsay, Jeanne Warren. *Pregnant Too Soon: Adoption Is an Option.* Rev. ed. 1987. Buena Park, Calif.: Morning Glory Press (0–930934–26–1); paper (0–930934–25–3). Ages 12–18.

"Adoption is chosen by less than 5 percent of all single teenage mothers in the United States," begins Lindsay, who feels strongly that a dearth of information on the subject stops young parents from considering adoption as an acceptable alternative to teen parenting. Here, she attempts to fill in some of the background. Coordinator of a California teen-mother program and author of a number of books about and for pregnant teens, Lindsay relies heavily on first-person testimony from parents in her program to get her message across. Young mothers readily share feelings about their decision to choose adoption and their varied experiences with agencies and adoptive parents. Woven throughout is information on adoption mechanics, foster-care placements, adoptive parental screening, rights of the birth mother, and more— little of which normally appears in teen pregnancy materials.

Lindsay, Jeanne Warren, and Jean Brunelli. *Teens Parenting—Your Pregnancy and Newborn Journey: How to Take Care of Yourself and Your Newborn if You're a Pregnant Teen.* 1991. Buena Park, Calif.: Morning Glory Press (0–930934–51–2); paper (0–930934–50–4). Ages 12–18.

Although teenagers can locate more specific information on this subject in Kitzinger's pregnancy book, it is in Lindsay and Brunelli's book that they'll find acknowledgment of some of their special

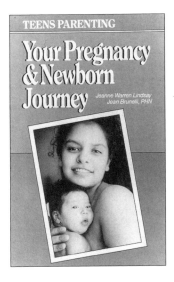

problems. The authors provide that recognition not only through numerous quotes they've collected from prospective and actual teenage parents but also through chapters addressing such topics as three-generation households. Part of the four book Teens Parenting series for pregnant and parenting teens (other books are listed in the following "Parenting" section), this is a wide-ranging sourcebook that touches on everything from prenatal care, labor, and delivery to a newborn's first days. Information on adoption is provided as is an understanding look at the dilemmas and responsibilities of expectant teen fathers. Unfortunately the subject coverage is uneven: for instance, the authors include a supportive discussion about breast feeding but little about bottle feeding. The section on birth control includes the new contraceptive implant but supplies only the briefest information about any of the methods it describes. The black-and-white photographs of teen parents and their babies will attract teen readers, though, and the friendly tone of the book will keep them reading.

Martin, Margaret. *The Illustrated Book of Pregnancy and Childbirth.* 1991. New York: Facts On File (0–8160–2570–3). Ages 13–up.

If explicit photographs of birth and fetal development such as those appearing in Kitzinger's books, cited previously, are unacceptable as a means of illustration, as they are in some communities, here's a book that can serve as a good alternative. Though its flowing, black-white-and-pink sketches are not particularly attractive, they are plentiful and extremely well labeled. They are also an integral part of this direct, well-ordered overview written by the founder of the Pregnancy and Natural Childbirth Education Center in Los Angeles. Martin begins by supplying some basic anatomical information, then follows the progress of baby and mother through the first week after birth. The book's open format and enlarged, spaciously set text (important terms are presented in extra-large type) is reminiscent of a children's book, but the text itself is neither patronizing nor oversimplified. Although teenagers who want to bottle feed won't find information here, Martin's text is otherwise a lucid description of what happens every step of the way.

Silverstein, Herma. *Teenage and Pregnant: What You Can Do.* 1988. Englewood Cliffs, N.J.: Messner (0–671–65221–4); paper (0–671–65222–2). Ages 13–17.

"The ideal time to have children is after you're married," writes Silverstein, who is up front about her feelings but still manages to provide important information to pregnant teens without sounding reproachful. She includes abortion among the options open to expectant mothers. Of the four choices, adoption, abortion, single parenting, and early marriage, she discusses adoption most thoroughly, devoting a whole chapter to summarizing its basic procedures and outlining the rights of the birth mother. In addition, she includes information on prenatal care, trimesterly development, and what to expect during labor and delivery. Like Lindsay and Brunelli, she also is attuned to the particular problems of pregnant teens and young mothers. Her style, however, is somewhat less accessible. Information on contraception and sexually transmitted diseases brings the no-nonsense book full circle.

Parenting

Caring for Your Baby and Young Child: Birth to Age Five. Edited by Stephen P. Shelov and others. 1991. New York: Bantam, paper (0–553–07186–6). Ages 14–up.

A description of the initial moments after birth introduces the first of a three-volume set intended to follow a child's development from birth to age 21. This book covers infancy through the pre-school years, and while it was published for adults, it is full of useful information for mothers of any age. Basic care concerns and an overview of the physical and emotional stages in a child's growth lead off, followed by a handy encyclopedic reference that includes information on emergency care, specific illnesses, and behavior problems. Here, too, is advice on everything from day-care facilities (teens may need one if they return to school or go to work) to helping a child cope with a death in the family. The book is wider in scope than

Leach's *Your Baby & Child* parenting manual. It is not, however, as congenially written.

Einon, Dorothy. *Parenthood: The Whole Story.* 1991. New York: Paragon (1–55778–374–8). Ages 14–up.

Although teenagers aren't used in the photographs here, and it's not to teenagers the author speaks, the information Einon has gathered is as important to expectant parents who are 15 or 16 as it is to those who are 30. Using an unusual system of clearly numbered paragraphs that facilitates cross-referencing, Einon details the processes of conception, pregnancy, and birth, considering the roles of both parents. She also introduces a variety of medical and emotional issues related to family planning and devotes nearly half her text to baby care. While she's more frank about parenting challenges than many books on the subject, she doesn't forget the joyful side of raising children. Teens will get a clear picture of both aspects of parenting. Neat drawings and diagrams are scattered throughout as are black-and-white photographs that record birth through babyhood.

Jessel, Camilla. *From Birth to Three.* 1991. New York: Dell/Delta, paper (0–385–30310–6). Ages 14–up.

"How soon will my baby roll over?" "When will my baby begin to talk?" "How soon will I see my baby smile?" To answer these and other common queries, Jessel offers a remarkable album of photographs, all of baby Lee, whose development she's captured in full-color candid pictures from the moment of his birth through his third year. Accompanied by informative captions, the photos record landmarks in Lee's physical and emotional growth and in the evolution of his speech, his socialization, and his learning and play patterns. Sidebars, color-keyed to each chapter, provide a background context for Lee's development that serves, in turn, as a flexible model of the changes most parents eventually will see in their babies. The text explores a baby's development in only the most general terms, but it is still a comforting look at the principal stages of child growth and a charming celebration of children.

Kitzinger, Sheila. *Breastfeeding Your Baby.* 1989. New York: Knopf, paper (0–679–72433–8). Ages 14–up.

Published for an adult audience but accessible to new mothers of a variety of ages, this attractively and abundantly illustrated book answers a pressing need for materials on the subject of breastfeeding. Photographs, many in full color, accompany Kitzinger's authoritative guidance on breast care and nursing basics, which she augments with reassurance and insight into infant development and the evolving relationship between parent and child. Kitzinger is also the author of *The Complete Book of Pregnancy and Childbirth,* listed previously in this chapter.

Landis, Dylan. *Checklist for Your New Baby.* 1991. New York: Putnam/Perigee, paper (0–399–51657–3). Ages 14–up.

With a bewildering array of products for babies on the market today, it's difficult to know what's necessary and what's not. Teen mothers, whose budgets are often restricted at best, need guidance as much as older parents do. Landis delivers it in a shopper's handbook devoted totally to infant supplies. Car seats, strollers, clothing, bath and nursing aids each have a chapter of their own, with Landis demonstrating her product knowledge by supplying consumer advice and safety tips. No brand names are used.

"I know some guys skip town or drop out of sight when they get a girl pregnant, but, man, I figure if you were there for the fun you ought to be there for the hard part, too."
Stanley, age 16
—from *Changing Bodies, Changing Lives*

Leach, Penelope. *Your Baby & Child: From Birth to Age Five.* Rev. ed. 1989. New York: Knopf (0–394–57951–8). Ages 14–up.

Of the many guides to child care and development, this one will be of particular interest to teenagers because of its straightforward style and copious illustration. Leach is encouraging and direct as she instructs parents and caregivers on children's developmental stages and provides basic information on how babies eat, learn, sleep, and adapt to new surroundings and situations. Covering newborns through pre-school age children, her book is a first-rate resource, made even more valuable by the extensive medical-emergency reference section that is appended.

Lindsay, Jeanne Warren. *Teens Parenting—The Challenge of Toddlers: Parenting Your Child from One to Three.* 1991. Buena Park, Calif.: Morning Glory Press (0–930934–59–8); paper (0–930934–58–X). Ages 12–18.

In the final volume in her four-part series (other volumes also listed in this chapter), Lindsay once again manages to be reassuring as well as truthful when it comes to the challenges of teenage parenting. Using a friendly tone that calls up visions of an experienced friend or concerned counselor, she picks up where *Teens Parenting: Your Baby's First Year,* described in a following citation, leaves off. Subjects touched upon range from sleep problems and temper tantrums to the importance of parent-child interaction. Loosely organized, topical chapters are catchalls of general advice and information, often presented without documentation ("Research shows that aggressive children tend to watch a lot of violence on television," for example). Lindsay pays more attention to teenage fathers than most parenting books, including a whole chapter on fathering, full of comments from young dads. In it she encourages even dads who don't live with their children to become involved parents. Lindsay contributes a strong sense of how children change parents' lives, strengthening her portrait with the first person comments of young people who speak about the satisfaction of parenting as well as its more onerous side. Her bibliography is too narrow given the wealth of resource material available on parenting concerns, but her book is still a genial overview that takes kids who have kids seriously.

Lindsay, Jeanne Warren, and Sally McCullough. *Teens Parenting— Discipline from Birth to Three: How to Prevent and Deal with Discipline Problems with Babies and Toddlers.* 1991. Buena Park, Calif.: Morning Glory Press (0–930934–55–5); paper (0–930934–54–7). Ages 12–18.

Writing with McCullough this time, Lindsay offers another in her four-book Teens Parenting series. Like others in the group,

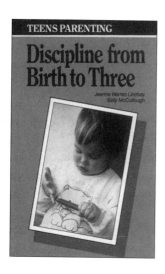

this book is organized in a loosely chronological fashion and highlights some common parenting dilemmas, in this case, problems that arise for the parents of children from newborn to age three. Steering caretakers away from spanking and shouting, the authors offer alternative strategies for dealing with particular problems such

as thumb sucking, toilet training, and tantrums, as well as ways to cope with the normal behavioral change of growing children. As is usual in Lindsay's books, comments from teenagers are scattered through the text, and special attention is paid to the problems experienced by teen parents, for example, the difficulty of asserting authority when grandparent caretakers disagree about discipline. Black-and-white photographs are scattered through the book.

Lindsay, Jeanne Warren. *Teens Parenting—Your Baby's First Year.* 1991. Buena Park, Calif.: Morning Glory Press (0–930934–53–9); paper (0–930934–52–0). Ages 12–18.

If readers can forgive the somewhat hit-or-miss approach (coverage is as uneven and selective here as it is in other books in the Teens Parenting series) and the annoyingly frequent references to other books in the series, this manual on baby care basics answers a nice variety of questions new parents have. Written in a pleasantly informal style that is enhanced by comments from young mothers and fathers, the text is a mixture of practical advice and information on infant health and development. As is usual in Lindsay's parenting books, practical information (in this case, discussions of diapers, immunizations, food, child-proofing a home, and age-appropriate toys) is accompanied by consideration of special teen-parent concerns, such as money problems, the importance of establishing paternity, and the need to return to school. Lindsay supplies more encouragement than answers about these problems, but she never attempts to fool her audience into thinking she's covering it all.

Miner, Jane Claypool. *Young Parents.* 1985. Englewood Cliffs, N.J.: Messner (0–671–49848–7). Ages 14–18.

A mother at 18 whose daughter is now grown, Miner predicts a difficult future for most young mothers, many of whom she feels will be unprepared or unwilling to accept the responsibilities parenting involves or make the sacrifices it demands.

She presents four options open to the unexpectedly pregnant—abortion, adoption, marriage, single parenting—revealing the difficulties teens will face in each situation. As the book title implies, however, she concentrates most on what being a teenage parent entails. She pays little attention to fathering in her discussions, but she does include a scattering of established child-rearing theory both parents can use. Unaffected comments from pregnant teens and young mothers lend credibility to the book and offset the author's somewhat formal tone.

Schnell, Barry T. *The Teenage Parent's Child Support Guide.* 1989. Yorklyn, Del.: Advocacy Center for Child Support, paper (0–910599–26–2). Ages 14–up.

In one of the few books on the subject accessible to teens, Schnell discusses social service assistance available to teenage parents, particularly mothers, and explains how they can get it for themselves and for their children. Noting that regulations and procedures may vary by state, he provides a few tips to help the application procedure go more smoothly and describes how to conquer specific problems teenagers often face when they confront the social services bureaucracy. He also includes information on obtaining emergency food and shelter, a discussion of court-established paternity, overviews of three of the more familiar welfare programs—AFDC (Aid to Families of Dependent Children), food stamps, and medicaid—and a brief look at pregnant students' rights. The questions and chapter summaries following each chapter suggest classroom application, but Schnell's friendly tone and encouragement make the text suitable for independent reading as well.

Silverstein, Herma. Teen Guide to Single Parenting. 1989. New York: Watts (0–531–10669–1). Ages 12–16.

Part of the Teen Guide series, Silverstein's text is a slim, attractively illustrated summary of its subject. It begins with a review of the special problems of single teen parents, among them getting financial support, dealing with loneliness, and finishing school. The author devotes most of her remaining text to baby care and child development concerns, providing practical suggestions for diapering, feeding, and disciplining that will be as useful to married as to single teen parents. While many more-comprehensive childcare books are available, Silverstein's is one of the few addressed to teens who have reading difficulties. Its brevity and appealing photographs may induce even teens who shy away from books to take a peek.

FICTION

Eyerly, Jeannette. *Someone to Love Me.* 1987. New York: Lippincott (0–397–32206–2). Ages 13–16.

What begins for Patrice as a love affair with the boy of her dreams turns into a nightmare when she becomes pregnant and her wonderful boyfriend disappears.

Klein, Norma. *No More Saturday Nights.* 1988. New York: Knopf (0–394–81944–6); Fawcett, paper (0–449–70304–5). Ages 15–18.

When he becomes an unwed father at the end of his senior year in high school and wins custody of his child, Tim Weber feels he has no choice but to take the baby with him to college in the fall.

Maguire, Jesse. *On the Edge.* 1991. New York: Ballantine, paper (0–8041–0447–6). Ages 15–18.

Eighteen-year-old Caroline discovers she's come out "on the wrong side of the birth control safety-rate statistics," and she has to make a choice between having her baby or having an abortion.

Myers, Walter Dean. *Sweet Illusion.* 1987. New York: Teachers & Writers Collaborative (0–915924–14–5); paper (0–915924–15–3). Ages 16–18.

In a book of fiction that reads like fact, a series of first-person narratives explore how inner city teens—mostly minority young men and women—grapple with decisions about pregnancy and deal with the problems of parenting.

Rylant, Cynthia. *A Kindness.* 1988. New York: Watts/Orchard/Richard Jackson (0–531–05767–4); Dell, paper (0–440–20579–4). Ages 14–18.

Chip has always had an especially close relationship with his single-parent mother Anne. Then Anne becomes pregnant, decides to raise the baby, and refuses to tell Chip who the father is.

Willey, Margaret. *If Not For You.* 1988. New York: Harper (0–06–026494–2); paper (0–06–447015–6). Ages 13–16.

Bonnie sees popular, pretty high school senior Linda Mason's elopement with Ray Pastrovich as a bid for independence as well as just about the most romantic thing she can imagine—until she becomes the couple's baby sitter and sees firsthand the difference between romance and real love.

Death:
Romance and Reality

THE DEATH OF a loved one is universally recognized as one of the most stressful occurrences in a person's life. Teenagers, in the throes of coping with sexual maturation, are especially vulnerable to death's emotional aftermath, which causes great upheaval in family and personal relationships. It also forces them to confront the scary thought of their own mortality. In this chapter are books that explore teenagers' feelings about dying. Included are titles that deal with how teenagers view the possibility of dying themselves or losing a loved one, as well as books that consider how they handle death when it actually occurs. That teenagers are frequently unable to see beyond the romantic images of death that are part of our cultural heritage is made painfully clear, often through the young peoples' own words.

"It's not surprising that the teen years are often filled with fear, loneliness, and insecurity. What *is* surprising is the fact that teenagers today seem less able or less willing to cope with the same changes and expectations their parents faced not so long ago."

—from *Dead Serious*

NONFICTION

Colman, Warren. *Understanding and Preventing Teen Suicide.* 1990. Chicago: Childrens Press (0–516–00594–4); paper (0–516–40594–2). Ages 12–15.

"There are always better ways than suicide to deal with despair," writes Colman, who explores what causes young people to opt out of life and what can be done to put them back on track. Facts are not documented, but the writing is clear. The author touches briefly on most of the vital aspects associated with his topic, using case histories and personal commentary without being exploitive. He also alerts readers to the signs that may presage suicide, but he cautions them clearly against taking on inappropriate responsibility. What makes the text different, however, is not the information it contains or even Colman's sensitivity; rather it's the book's well-chosen color illustrations and spacious format, both of which make reading about a particularly difficult topic much easier.

Gravelle, Karen, and Charles Haskins. *Teenagers Face to Face with Bereavement.* 1989. Englewood Cliffs, N.J.: Messner (0–671–65856–5); paper (0–671–65975–8). Ages 12–18.

Gravelle, a former psychotherapist, and Haskins, an Episcopal priest and pastoral counselor, supply the context for the moving testimonies of seventeen young people. Ranging in age from 10 to 18 at the time of their loss, the teenagers mourn friends, parents, brothers, and sisters. The teenagers unpretentiously communicate their feelings in chapters that distinguish the stages of grief as they particularly affect the young—how it feels to return to school after the funeral, how friends help, and how roles change in a family after a parent's death. Painful emotions—denial, confusion, guilt—reverberate through the text, making the book difficult to read. But by gathering and sharing these emotions, the authors give shape to the devastation of personal loss in a way that will help teenage survivors of similar traumas feel less isolated in their grief.

Hermes, Patricia. *A Time to Listen: Preventing Youth Suicide.* San Diego: HBJ (0–15–288196–4). Ages 13–18.

While Hermes does include information about suicide and advice on what to do should a reader suspect a friend or loved one of being in suicidal crisis, she is more successful defining the emotions surrounding suicide than presenting the factual underpinnings of the tragedy. Through informal interviews with individuals who attempted suicide, bereaved parents and friends, a therapist, and a group of teenagers concerned about the suicide of a peer, she sheds light on the social and personal implications of the act. Her question-answer technique is awkward at times, but the voices of her subjects break through as does a sense of the internal and external pressures teenagers face everyday.

"I think a lot of them think about glamorizing their own funeral—who will be there to mourn, and what it will be like and how sorry everyone will be. And there's some sense of reaping the benefit of that sorrow. As if they'll be back to be treated differently." Dr. Eleanor Craig
—from *A Time to Listen*

Kolehmainen, Janet, and Sandra Handwerk. *Teen Suicide: A Book for Friends, Family, and Classmates.* 1986. Minneapolis: Lerner (0–8225–0037–X); paper (0–8225–9514–1). Ages 11–14.

The authors alert readers to the eight classic warning signals of suicide and suggest ways they can find help for someone they feel may be suicidal. They begin by correcting common misconceptions: that people who threaten suicide won't actually do it; that suicidal individuals are crazy; that someone who is suicidal will never be well again. A series of vignettes then illuminate the emotional issues facing suicide survivors and friends of teens who have killed themselves. In one story a boy tries to help a friend who's attempted suicide ease back into school life; in another, a girl wrestles with the guilt she feels after a friend who expressed a suicidal wish is placed in a psychiatric hospital by worried parents.

Krementz, Jill. *How It Feels When a Parent Dies.* 1981.
New York: Knopf, paper
(0–394–75855–2).
Ages 11–15.

Published more than a decade ago and the prototype for the author's How It Feels series, this was one of the first children's books to recognize a young person's need to express and discuss his or her feelings about a parent's death. Eighteen young people, coping with a mother's or father's death by suicide, accident, or illness, told Krementz their stories, and their heartfelt admissions are every bit as powerful and affecting now as they were all those years ago. Authentic in tone, thanks to Krementz's adept editing, the recollections express the confusion, anger, and guilt kids feel when tragedy strikes. They also reveal a variety of thought-provoking beliefs about what happens when a person dies. Though filled with painful details, these are ultimately triumphant accounts of kids who've grieved and survived. What they reveal may help both children and adults facing difficult times. Black-and-white photographs, including at least one portrait of each young person, bring the documentary to life.

"We see death every day on television—and we think, oh, he got shot, well, he'll be back the next day. And even the songs on the radio. There's one of them that starts off, 'Sometimes you're better off dead, there's a gun in your hand and it's pointed at your head.'" Richard Klein, suicide survivor

—from *A Time to Listen*

Langone, John. *Dead End: A Book about Suicide.* 1986. Boston: Little, Brown (0–316–51432–2). Ages 13–18.

Langone strikes a near equal balance between personal commentary from teenagers and perspectives from medical professionals. The book poses important questions to readers while it relays facts and information. Quotes from young adults introduce each of the chapters, which delve into the biological, sociological, historic, and behavioral aspects of suicide. A strong advocate of suicide prevention programs in schools and communities, Langone censures school officials, parents, and government agencies for thinking "as though they believe that if they don't talk about it, it will go away." He devotes a section to describing what he feels can and should be done to bring discussion of suicide into the open, where he feels it belongs. In terms of individual guidance, he explains how someone in a suicidal crisis can be helped and offers words of comfort and understanding to teens who are themselves struggling with self-destructive feelings.

Leder, Jane Mersky. *Dead Serious: A Book for Teenagers about Teenage Suicide.* 1987. New York: Atheneum (0–689–31262–8); Avon, paper (0–380–70661–X). Ages 13–18.

"Kids who threaten suicide aren't interested in ending their lives. They're interested in ending their pain," writes Leder, who frankly discusses the causes, the fallacies and facts, and the warning signs of suicide among teens as well as the ramifications of the act on surviving family and friends. Avoiding stuffy textbook jargon, she speaks directly to her readers, infusing her text with interviews, case studies, and lengthy scenarios, some including dialogue, to make her subject more relevant and compelling. She stresses that adult intervention is a necessity during a suicidal crisis, but she also recognizes that friends can play an important role in identifying a teenager at risk. Addressing individuals who are concerned about someone they know, she explains how to spot signs of trouble and become better listeners and more supportive friends, even when that means betraying a confidence by contacting a parent or a teacher, or calling a suicide hotline.

"We all think about death at certain times, but I swear I never thought I'd have to think about it right after my 18th birthday. Being a teenager is hellish anyway. Drop AIDS into the picture and it becomes all the more confusing." David, age 18

—from *Risky Times*

Richter, Elizabeth. *Losing Someone You Love: When a Brother or Sister Dies.* 1986. New York: Putnam (0–399–21243–4). Ages 11–14.

Photographs taken by the author picture young people of various races and ages who talk about the death of a brother or sister. Presented without comment from Richter, their statements are simple and immediate. The young people speak about their relationship with their brother or sister and explain what happened and how they're coping. Anger, jealousy, and guilt are often found alongside heartfelt expressions of grief and loss. Some of the young people comment on the funeral, some on altered relationships in their families; all stress the importance of talking about feelings with a therapist or a friend. "It's going to be sad for a long time," says one, "but you will eventually be able to deal with it and get your life back in order." This is a quiet, sensitive book that will help readers who've experienced family loss as well as those who are concerned about the subjects of death or bereavement from a broader perspective.

Rofes, Eric E., ed. The Unit at Fayerweather Street School. *The Kids' Book about Death and Dying: By and for Kids.* 1985.

Boston: Little, Brown (0–316–75390–4). Ages 11–13.

Death was the topic chosen for children involved in a year-long discussion group at a New England independent school. With guidance from their teacher, the students, ages 11 to 14, interviewed people of many ages, visited hospitals and funeral homes, and read books and poetry about dying. This book presents what they learned. Divided first into broad, well-ordered chapters on such matters as funeral customs, the death of a loved one, and the loss of a pet, the material later breaks into specific topics: euthanasia, organ donation, cremation, wills. Statistics on the life spans of various animals are provided, and the stages of grieving are explained, as are the stages of accepting one's own dying. A moving chapter containing comments from fatally ill children and their siblings is included as well. Strong throughout are the voices of the students involved in the discussion group, which express varied beliefs as the children try to come to grips with an experience they found both "serious and sad."

FICTION

Crutcher, Chris. *Stotan!* 1986. New York: Greenwillow (0–685–05715–2); Dell, paper (0–440–20080–6). Ages 15–18.

The ties that bind four teenage friends grow tighter as they see each other through personal crises, including the discovery that one of the group is dying of a rare blood disease.

Deaver, Julie Reece. *Say Goodnight, Gracie.* 1988. New York: Harper (0–06–021418–X); paper (0–06–447007–5). Ages 14–18.

Morgan Hackett and Jimmy Woolf have grown up side by side. Loving friends, verbal sparring partners, and confidants, they are interdependent in innumerable ways. Then Jimmy is killed in an automobile accident, and Morgan must learn to face life without him.

Ellis, Sarah. *A Family Project*. 1988. New York: Macmillan/Margaret K. McElderry (0–689–50444–6). Ages 11–14.

Mum is pregnant, and 11-year-old Jessica is so excited she decides to study babies instead of monotremes for her school science project. Finally, the long-awaited baby Lucie arrives, only to become a tiny victim of crib death.

Ferris, Jean. *Invincible Summer*. 1987. New York: Farrar (0–374–33642–3); Avon, paper (0–380–70619–9). Ages 14–18.

When Robin Gregory is diagnosed with leukemia, her loving father cannot cope. Her plucky grandmother stays by her side, but it's fellow leukemia patient Rick Winn—first her friend, then her secret lover—who teaches her about hope and courage.

Grant, Cynthia. *Phoenix Rising; Or How to Survive Your Life*. 1989. New York: Atheneum (0–689–31458–2). Ages 14–18.

Petulant, wisecracking Jesse can't seem to adjust to her sister Helen's recent death. What eventually helps her to overcome her grief is reading Helen's journal.

Hamilton, Virginia. *Cousins*. 1990. New York: Putnam/Philomel (0–399–22164–6). Ages 11–14.

Eleven-year-old Cammy hates her goody-goody cousin who makes fun of Cammy's beloved Gram. But when Cammy wishes Patty Ann dead and the wish actually comes true, Cammy's sorrow and guilt are almost too much to bear.

Irwin, Hadley. *So Long at the Fair*. 1988. New York: Macmillan/Margaret K. McElderry (0–0689–50454–3). Ages 14–18.

Unable to forget his beautiful friend Ashley who committed suicide at the fairgrounds, Joel changes his name and takes a job at the state fair. When his new friends react with anger on learning his real identity, he at last lets himself face the fact of Ashley's death. In remembering, he learns to let go of the past.

Kerr, M. E. *Night Kites*. 1986. New York: Harper (0–06–023253–6); paper (0–06–447035–0). Ages 15–18.

In the midst of an affair with a kookie, sexy classmate, Erick learns that his older brother Pete has AIDS and wants to come home to die.

Naughton, Jim. *My Brother Stealing Second*. 1989. New York: Harper (0–06–024374–0). Ages 14–18.

Since his baseball-star brother's death in a drunk-driving accident, Bobby Connely can't bring himself to return to his own beloved ball team.

Peck, Richard. *Remembering the Good Times*. 1985. New York: Delacorte (0–385–29396–8); Dell, paper (0–440–97339–2). Ages 14–18.

Buck, Kate, and Travis have been friends since junior high, even though their home lives and backgrounds are very different. When Travis kills himself, Buck remembers the good times the three had together. He also realizes how little he really understood his friend.

Pevsner, Stella. *How Could You Do It, Diane?* 1989. New York: Clarion (0–395–51041–4). Ages 12–14.

Bethany discovers her older stepsister dead from a barbiturate overdose. Though her parents refuse to deal openly with the tragedy, Bethany decides to put her own grief to rest by learning more about why Diane chose to die.

Thesman, Jean. *Last April Dancers*. 1987. New York: Houghton (0–395–403024–0); paper (0–380–70614–8). Ages 12–16.

When Catherine's gentle father kills himself on her sixteenth birthday, she blames her mother, her grandmother, and especially herself for causing his death.

A Filmography

Compiled by Ellen Mandel

MOST OF TODAY'S YOUNG ADULTS have been raised with TV. "Sesame Street" taught them numbers and letters, and media advertisements molded their tastes and attitudes. As a result, many teens absorb facts from a TV screen more readily than from a book's pages. When their minds are distracted by serious crises, young people may have even more difficulty concentrating on reading. A TV drama can offer escape from life's concerns while simultaneously counseling, consoling, and advising.

The following list represents some of the best current videos (most released within the last three to five years) available to young people facing personal challenges. Including both documentaries and dramatizations, the selections are suitable for home and school viewing; many are accompanied by study guides to enhance their classroom applications. Age levels are suggested. A variety of factors were considered in determining them, including subject matter, running time, and ages of the characters. Unlike videos that are released solely for home entertainment, these titles are very expensive. Large public libraries and school districts may own some of them; other programs may be accessible through public and school library film and video cooperatives. Cited prices are for the VHS format, and rental prices, when known, have been included to facilitate short-term rental of prints from distributors. Prices and addresses are current as of the time of this book's publication.

In compiling this list, I have consulted respected video selection tools. Mostly, however, I have called upon my fourteen years' experience as an assistant editor of nonprint materials for *Booklist*. I also relied upon and appreciate the input of my former *Booklist* colleagues.

While the majority of listed titles focus on one particular topic and are keyed to specific chapters in this book, the following three successful series of programs cover a wide range of teen concerns, from friendship, dating, and pregnancy to racism, substance abuse, and physical disabilities.

Degrassi Junior High, Term 1, 2 & 3. 1987–88. 42 episodes. Each program, 30 min., guides. Ages 11–14.

Degrassi High School, Term 4. 1989; released 1990. 15 episodes. Each program, 30 min., guides. Ages 14–18.

Degrassi High School, Term 5. 1991. 12 episodes: 1 program, 60 min.; 11 programs, 30 min., guides. Ages 14–18.

Direct Cinema, P.O. Box 10003, Santa Monica, CA 90410. Each program, $250. Rental, $25 per title.

With provocative plots attuned to the realities of teens' lives and subplots that intensify viewer interest, the programs in all of these critically acclaimed series center around a group of ethnically diverse Degrassi neighborhood kids. The *Degrassi Junior High* series was originally broadcast on television in the 1980s. The 1990s find the kids have progressed to high school. *Degrassi High School, Term 4* and *Term 5,* realistically tackle contemporary teen issues.

Wednesday's Children. The Media Guild, 11722 Sorrento Valley Rd., San Diego, CA 92121. 1989. Six programs. Each 14-15 min., guides. Each program, $210. Ages 14–adult.

This impressive six-part series dramatizes teens at risk from peer pressure, sexual abuse, dysfunctional families, absentee parents, and loneliness. Skilled acting and directing together with commanding plots involve viewers in the series' thought-provoking, open-ended vignettes.

FAMILY MATTERS

The Crown Prince. The Media Guild, 11722 Sorrento Valley Rd., San Diego, CA 92121. 1988; released 1990. 38 min., guide, $345. Ages 11–up.

Fifteen-year-old Billy and his younger brother, Freddy, hide in their rooms while their father physically and verbally abuses their mother. Billy wants to guard this tragic family secret, but Freddy tells the school authorities. Before the mother and her sons take refuge at a local shelter, Billy begins to exhibit violent behavior and is horrified to realize he may be growing up to be like his dad.

Daddy Can't Read. AIMS Media, 9710 DeSoto Ave., Chatsworth, CA 91311. 1988; released 1990. 45 min., $99.95. Rental, $50. Ages 11–up.

Although she donates her time to a high school literacy program, Allison Watson does not realize her own father cannot read. When she learns the truth, she encourages and finally persuades him to attend night school. This effectively worked drama meaningfully conveys the fears and feelings of inadequacy one man experiences because of illiteracy and depicts the power of a concerned and caring family that helps the man help himself.

Families in Trouble: Learning to Cope. Sunburst Communications, 39 Washington Ave., Pleasantville, NY 10570. 1990. 35 min., guide, $199. Ages 12–18.

Three situations of family crises—child abuse, parental fighting, and teenage alcoholism—are shown to have an impact on teens in the family. Even though young adults in these troubled families may not be directly involved in the incidents, they often feel responsible. Information provided about counseling and other positive coping strategies will reassure and help guide affected viewers.

Just for the Summer. Churchill
    Films, 12210 Nebraska Ave.,
    Los Angeles, CA 90025. 1990.
    29 min., guide, $295. Rental, $60.
    Ages 13–18.

High school track star Philip is an outgoing teen who suffers when his grandmother comes to live with his family. Grandmother's often unpredictable and irrational behavior, caused by Alzheimer's disease, frustrates and confuses Philip and causes tension for everyone. This poignant dramatization depicts the effects of Alzheimer's from a teen perspective.

Necessary Parties. Public Media
    Video (Wonderworks),
    5597 N. Ravenswood,
    Chicago, IL 60640. 1988;
    released 1990. 110 min.,
    $29.95. Ages 11–14.

When his parents announce their plans to divorce, Chris Mills decides to sue them. The teenager, who has looked after his kid sister through the years of their parents' stormy marriage, turns for counsel to an auto mechanic friend with a law degree. In a realistic portrayal of suburban junior high life, children's feelings about their parents' divorce—especially their desire to prevent dissolution of the marriage—come to light. The reasonable price is a bonus. Adapted from the novel *Necessary Parties,* by Barbara Dana (Harper, 1987).

Nobody's Home. FilmFair Communi-
    cations, 10621 Magnolia Blvd.,
    North Hollywood, CA 91601.
    1990. 20 min., guide, $385.
    Rental, $45. Ages 12–up.

A patient, effective school social worker slowly wins the trust of 10-year-old Anthony and draws from the troubled child the fact that he is responsible for looking after a younger brother while their mother is away from home working or dating. The unkempt, nervous Anthony is helped to understand his strong feelings about the neglect he endures, and the skilled social worker motivates positive changes in the boys' home situation. This is a fine dramatization of a very prevalent type of child abuse.

Teens in Changing Families:
    Making It Work.
    Sunburst Communications,
    39 Washington Ave.,
    Pleasantville, NY 10570. 1989.
    25 min., guide, $169.
    Ages 12–up.

The guilt and conflicting loyalties experienced by teenagers who have both biological and stepparents; the adjustments necessary to live in two homes—one where parents are strict, the other where parents are lenient and even indulgent; and the resentment of discipline imposed by a "wicked" stepparent are among the controversies aired in candid discussions with teens and parents from blended families. Group counseling and family meetings are shown to pave the road to understanding and improved relationships for these "instant" families.

Why Does Mom Drink So Much?
    Human Relations Media,
    175 Tompkins Ave.,
    Pleasantville, NY 10570.
    1989. 30 min., guide, $189.
    Rental, $40. Ages 14–18.

The painful emotions of shame, anger, and loneliness tear at children of alcoholic parents, often driving these youngsters to drink or to pursue other self-destructive escapes. This caring production urges teens to realize they have no control over their parents' drinking. The personal experiences candidly shared by young people with alcoholic parents along with helpful comments from professionals attest to the value of support groups for comfort and guidance.

SCHOOL DAZE

Dropping Out: Road to Nowhere.
Guidance Associates,
Communications Park,
Box 3000, Mount Kisco,
NY 10549. 1988. 60 min.,
guide, $209. Ages 13–up.

As society becomes more technologically specialized, there is less opportunity for unskilled workers and high school dropouts to find jobs. The testimonies of teens who left school or graduated with minimal training reinforce dismal, documented facts about these laborers' employment and earning potentials. This worthwhile program that encourages young people to stay in school also shows scenes from some alternative urban schools that teach life skills and promote self-worth.

*Life After High School:
Manufacturing Workers.* Pyramid
Film & Video, Box 1048,
Santa Monica, CA 90406.
1990. 29 min., guide, $295.
Rental, $95. Ages 14–18.

A tour of a candle company innovatively attempting to alleviate worker boredom and of a bindery where a plant worker compares the work-day grind with carefree high school days-gone-by are part of this provocative program that prods high schoolers to think about their futures. A variety of other workers—skilled, unskilled, and professional—also are featured.

ME, MYSELF, AND I

*Learning to be Assertive—The Basic
Skills: When Saying No Is Not
Enough.* 1987. 27 min.

*Learning to be Assertive—Advanced
Skills.* 1987; released 1989.
21 min.

AIMS Media, 9710 DeSoto Ave.,
Chatsworth, CA 91311. Each
program, $395. Rental, $75 per
title. Ages 13–15.

Young adults usually are more willing to take advice from their peers than from their parents or other adults. With that in mind, these productions feature teen hosts helping viewers through the skirmishes of daily life by demonstrating and reinforcing assertiveness skills. Whether the concerns addressed be minor situations of sibling stress, serious decisions regarding sexuality and drugs, or complex predicaments requiring skilled communication with harried teachers or even with an intoxicated parent, this excellent pair of programs provides teens with the assertive communication skills needed to cope successfully.

The Perfect Date. FilmFair
Communications, 10621 Magnolia
Blvd., North Hollywood,
CA 91601. 1990. 45 min.,
guide, $395. Rental, $40.
Ages 13–18.

Too often teens focus on being the "best." Stephen wants to be the school basketball star, and he wants to snare a date with the homecoming queen. He realizes both these goals. Then, in a series of humorous mishaps, he is stood up by his dream girl, loses his father's car to a tow truck, and finds Bernice, whose sincerity and charm make her a far more attractive date than the homecoming queen.

The Power of Choice. Live Wire
Video Publishers, 3315
Sacramento St., San Francisco,
CA 94118. 1987. 58 min., $79.95.
Ages 13–up.

Much more than an entertaining comedian, Michael Pritchard is a first-rate discussion leader and rapt listener—talents honed while working as a juvenile counselor. In scenes capturing his informal encounters with teens and his performances before high school audiences, Pritchard amusingly and effectively advises young adults to formulate clear goals, take positive initiative, and keep things in proper perspective. His unique approach helps young people eye life with a sense of humor, while his advice inspires them to work toward their ambitions.

Supermom's Daughter. The Media Guild, 11722 Sorrento Valley Rd., San Diego, CA 92121. 1987; released 1989. 32 min., $345. Ages 12–up.

Noelle's high-powered career mom cannot understand her daughter's desire to study early childhood education, especially since Noelle is a brilliant science student. Despite her parent's pressure to choose a more sophisticated college major, Noelle holds to her convictions, showing how she can combine her knack for science with her love of children by inventing a robot "monster buster" to chase away children's nightmares. A professionally polished, well-acted, and meaningful drama, this speaks to teens' need to find their own path in life.

Surviving in the Real World. Human Relations Media, 175 Tompkins Ave., Pleasantville, NY 10570. 1991. Three programs, each 25–32 min., guides. Each program, $169–$199. Rental, $40 per title. Ages 15–18.

Available individually, the selections in this trio of videos advise older teens about some of the practicalities of living independently. *Dollars and Sense* discusses checking accounts, budgeting, obtaining credit, and maintaining a savings program. *Housing and Transportation* helps young adults buy a car and find an apartment. *Lifestyle* encompasses such everyday essentials as insurance, food and clothes, education, and time management.

Ten Easy Ways to Lose Your Job. Human Relations Media, 175 Tompkins Ave., Pleasantville, NY 10570. 1990. 25 min., guide, $189. Rental, $40. Ages 14–18.

First-time teenage workers may think they can give merchandise away to their friends or call in sick when they'd rather not go to work. This lighthearted, informative production helps them view their jobs from the boss's perspective as it stresses the need for employee responsibility, honesty, and dependability.

CRACK, GLUE, OR A SIX-PACK OR TWO?

Bulking Up: The Dangers of Steroids. AIMS Media, 9710 DeSoto Ave., Chatsworth, CA 91311. 1990. 23 min., $395. Rental, $75. Ages 14–up.

Congenially hosted by Olympic medalist Bruce Jenner, this informative documentary nonthreateningly discourages steroid use. In addition to citing the litany of potential steroid side effects, the program hears from such appealing role models as an NFL trainer, a former NFL football player, a body builder, and retired Olympic athletes to make its case against steroid abuse.

Crack U.S.A.: Country Under Siege. Ambrose Video Publishing, 1290 Avenue of the Americas, New York, NY 10104. 1989. 42 min., $99.95. Ages 13–up.

Crack cocaine is one of the most addictive, dangerous, and available street drugs. This frightening documentary underscores those realities. It reveals how crack has hooked seemingly innocent youngsters in its pervasive invasion of American culture, epitomized by what has happened in Palm Beach County, Florida.

Dare to be Different: Resisting Drug-Related Peer Pressure. Guidance Associates, Communications Park, Box 3000, Mount Kisco, NY 10549. 1988. 19 min., guide, $59. Ages 12–15.

Kim and Sarah are relay racers and friends, but they take different tracks when Kim is attracted to a drinking and drug-abusing crowd. Ultimately, Kim grows bored with her new acquaintances and their one-dimensional interests and returns to racing. A well-produced drama, this video addresses self-esteem and the value of friendship as well as the dangers of substance abuse.

Early Warning Signs: Recognizing the Signs of Addiction. MTI Film & Video, 108 Wilmot Rd., Deerfield, IL 60015. 1991. 21 min., guide, $350. Rental, $75. Ages 12–up.

In this sincere, caring dramatization, families of addicts, gathered in a drug-rehab waiting room, talk about how they failed to recognize their loved ones' addictions. Through flashbacks, family members recall the denial, anger, and hostility that go hand-in-hand with addiction. Addiction's warning signs are clearly summarized in the production, which informs as it sensitizes viewers to the needs and suffering of addicts and their families.

The Morning After: A Story of Vandalism. Pyramid Film & Video, Box 1048, Santa Monica, CA 90406. 1989; released 1990. 27 min., guide, $325. Rental, $75. Ages 12–18.

While under the influence of alcohol, four Minnesota youths broke into the local high school and savagely vandalized it, causing one million dollars in damage. The teens try to explain their rampage to viewers, but the effects of their irrational violence, documented by newsreel footage, speak louder than words about the impact of peer pressure and alcohol abuse.

Over the Limit. FilmFair Communications, 10621 Magnolia Blvd., North Hollywood, CA 91601. 1990. 45 min., guide, $395. Rental, $40. Ages 12–18.

After a drunk driving accident leaves several of his friends dead, Matt determines to find out the truth about who was driving their wrecked van. In the process, Matt and the viewer learn to distinguish between memories and being honest and loyal to friends. Additionally, this reworking of Todd Strasser's novel *The Accident* (Doubleday, 1988) reinforces the dangers of driving drunk.

Stop Before You Drop. Durrin Productions, 1748 Kalorama Rd.

NW, Washington, DC 20009. 1988; released 1989. 12 min., guide, $205. Rental, $52. Ages 9–up.

"Fight it. . . . Don't light it" is the catchy refrain in a talented rapper's performance that advises viewers to resist peer pressure and alluring advertising. The lyrics also give reasons not to smoke and offer suggestions for kicking the habit.

PRIVATE PROPERTY: DON'T TOUCH!

Abby, My Love. FilmFair Communications, 10621 Magnolia Blvd., North Hollywood, CA 91601. 1991. 45 min., guide, $395. Rental, $40. Ages 15–up.

Chip Wilson and Abby Gilmore have known each other since childhood. Now in high school, the pair find their affection deepening. But Abby is afraid to commit herself to more than friendship. Chip finally finds out why when a distraught Abby reveals that her father has been sexually abusing her for years. Good editing, fine acting, and the utmost discretion characterize a dramatic depiction of the worst and best in human relationships.

Date Rape: Violence Among Friends. American School Publishers, P.O. Box 4520, Chicago, IL 60680. 1991. 22 min., guide, $63. Ages 14–18.

The comments of a rape-crisis professional and interviews with two young women who were raped by men they knew help illuminate the trauma of date rape. In addition to heightening awareness, this production primes viewers to recognize and to prevent potentially threatening situations and offers guidelines for recovery to those who have suffered sexual abuse.

WELLNESS

Fighting Back: Teenage Depression. Sunburst Communications, 39 Washington Ave., Pleasantville,

NY 10570. 1991. 44 min.,
guide, $199. Ages 14–18.

In excellently acted vignettes, three young adults display characteristic signs of serious depression brought on by true-to-life crises. In one instance a girl has broken up with her boyfriend; in another, a boy is pressured to attend a prestigious college against his will; in the third, a young woman is forced to babysit for her younger siblings instead of living her own life. All three receive helpful intervention from professionals who legitimize the teens' feelings and counsel them toward emotional well-being.

Gambler. FilmFair Communications,
10621 Magnolia Blvd., North
Hollywood, CA 91601. 1990.
45 min., guide, $395. Rental, $40.
Ages 13–up.

Seventeen-year-old Jim is an honor student and star quarterback on his high school football team. Colleges already are wooing him. But he gambles away his promising prospects by compulsively betting on professional football games. Only after his preoccupation with debts and with gambling take their toll on his grades, cause him to be benched from the team, and cost him his girlfriend and most of the possessions he holds dear do his parents learn the truth. Then Jim begins to get the help he needs to recover. A gripping portrayal of an increasingly serious problem among today's youth.

High on Life: Feeling Good Without
Drugs. Guidance Associates,
Communications Park, Box 3000,
Mount Kisco, NY 10549.
1988. 46 min., guide, $209.
Ages 12–18.

Eight students tell how outlets such as wheelchair athletics, motocross, and rock climbing led them to "natural highs" as opposed to drug-induced highs. Despite their own health and emotional crises, these personable youths have discovered positive ways to set goals and to offset discouragement. Their lively testimonies will inspire others to find enthusiasm in life

rather than trying to escape problems through drugs.

A Season in Hell. New Day Films,
121 W. 27th St., #902, New York,
NY 10001. 1989; released 1991.
59 min., guide, $395. Rental, $70.
Ages 15–up.

Representative media hype about ideal feminine bodies adeptly interplays with interviews, conducted over a five-year period, with Regina Hatfield and her family in a program that poignantly reveals the influences behind young Regina's eating disorder. A personal look at the anguish caused by Regina's obsession with food and her looks, this production movingly documents the effects of bulimia.

Self-defeating Behavior: How to Stop
It. 1990. 40 min., guide.

Stress Reduction Strategies That
Really Work! 1990. 31 min.,
guide. Human Relations Media,
175 Tompkins Ave., Pleasantville,
NY 10570.

Each program, $189. Rental, $40
each. Ages 14–18.

In a stimulating seminar format, both of these titles deliver practical advice on how to respond to typical teen situations. In the first program, problem assessment and self-diagnosis, techniques for controlling negative thinking, and behavioral strategies are recommended to counter social anxiety, worry, lack of assertiveness, and procrastination. Time management, assertiveness, and relaxation techniques are among the remedies promoted in the second program.

SEX STUFF

Boy Stuff. Churchill Films, 12210
Nebraska Ave., Los Angeles, CA
90025. 1986. 16 min., guide,
$270. Rental, $60. Ages 10–14.

Humor takes the edge off adolescent boys' self-consciousness as well as their concerns about maturation and embarrassments such as body odor and spontaneous erections.

Honest facts supportively inform viewers about the personal hygiene practices they'll need to follow.

Condoms: A Responsible Option. Landmark Films, 3450 Slade Run Dr., Falls Church, VA 22042. 1991. 10 min., guide, $195. Rental, $50. Ages 16–up.

A couple's intimate evening is interrupted by the uninvited arrival of their previous sexual partners, followed by the arrival of the previous partners' previous partners. The resulting roomful of sexually active adults clearly illustrates the narrator's advice about the role of condoms in combating the spread of sexually transmitted diseases such as AIDS. This almost slapstick episode may be the lure that draws older teens' attention to the effective use of condoms and helps them understand the necessity of protection for both women and men. Originally released in 1987, the film has been updated to include additional information on latex condoms and AIDS.

Dr. Sol Gordon: A Test of Love. Public Films, P.O. Box 1689, Wimberley, TX 78676. 1986; released 1987. 28 min., $165. Ages 14–18.

Speaking in his usual flamboyant but forthright style, author and educator Sol Gordon is seen at one of his frequent addresses before a high school audience. Though AIDS is not mentioned, Gordon does not shy away from other topics of frequent teenage concern, such as masturbation, homosexuality, and sexual abuse. Offering arguments to counter sexual pressuring, he strongly advocates that young adults abstain from sex and cites statistics about teenage pregnancies and STDs to support his position. For teens who choose to be sexually active, he promotes contraceptives. A dynamic speaker on vital issues, he gives teenagers something to think about.

Facts About AIDS. AIMS Media, 9710 DeSoto Ave., Chatsworth, CA 91311. 1990. 11 min., $250. Rental, $75. Ages 15–up.

Up-to-date and accurate, this production provides a compact, yet comprehensive, explanation of AIDS. Defining the disease, clarifying how it can and cannot be transmitted, and discussing therapy and prevention, the program effectively conveys life-saving information to teens—a group at great risk for contracting AIDS in the years ahead.

Girl Stuff. Churchill Films, 12210 Nebraska Ave., Los Angeles, CA 90025. 1982. 21 min., guide, $330. Ages 10–14.

The comments of preadolescent and young teenage girls combine with a pleasing mix of animation and advertisements to help blossoming young women distinguish between media hype and their real physical and emotional needs. This well-produced common-sense approach to reproductive maturity and its attendant necessities of personal hygiene comfortably promotes a positive self-image.

The Great Chastity Experiment. The Media Guild, 11721 Sorrento Valley Rd., San Diego, CA 92121. 1985; released 1986. 27 min., $245. Rental, $50. Ages 14–18.

When teens Nicki and Keith decide to try chastity for one week, they find that getting to know each other's true personalities, intellects, interests, and feelings can be harder than having sex. But after a week of quick kisses only, the couple extend their experiment for another week. This slick, made-for-TV drama is certain to cause teens to consider the quality and direction of their relationships.

Just a Regular Kid: An AIDS Story. The Media Guild, 11722 Sorrento Valley Rd., San Diego, CA 92121. 1987; released 1989. 34 min., guide, $345. Ages 12–18.

Attacking the fears and misconceptions that surround AIDS, this TV drama tells of Kevin, a high school youth who contracts the virus from a blood transfusion. Initially Kevin is ostracized by his classmates, including his best friend, Paul. But in the program's pat conclusion, Paul advocates for Kevin and heightens AIDS awareness among his fellow students and among viewers. Adapted from the novel *Goodbye Tomorrow,* by Gloria Miklowitz (Delacorte, 1987).

*Sexual Orientation: Reading
   Between the Labels.*
   NEWIST/CESA #7, 1110 IS
   Bldg. UWGB, Green Bay, WI
   54301. 1991. 28 min.,
   guide, $195. Rental, $50.
   Ages 13–up.

Hosted by a congenial young man named Jeff, this top-notch program mixes insightful comments from parents and professionals with the frankly spoken words of gay and lesbian teenagers to explain the pressures gay youth face today and the various ways they handle their problems.

Teen Contraception. AIMS Media,
   9710 DeSoto Ave., Chatsworth,
   CA 91311. 1989; released 1990.
   13 min., $250. Rental, $75.
   Ages 14–18.

In a nonthreatening manner, an unbiased teen host informs peers about the female reproductive system and cycle and about birth control methods. Commonly held yet often dangerous myths about sexuality and pregnancy are dispelled by this valuable program's explanations. The film is also available in Spanish.

Too Far Too Fast. Film Ideas,
   3575 Commercial Ave.,
   Northbrook, IL 60062. 1989.
   26 min., guide, $189.
   Rental, $60. Ages 14–18.

While it focuses on two couples, this comprehensive production incorporates a panorama of teen attitudes about sexuality. Melissa and Josh are at odds over how far to go sexually, while Angie and Hector suspect they've already gone too far— Angie might be pregnant. Some of their friends talk silliness; others talk sense. As this realistic drama unfolds, the teens grow in maturity and understanding.

The Truth About Alex. Coronet/MTI
   Film & Video, 108 Wilmot Rd.,
   Deerfield, IL 60015. 1988;
   released 1989. 49:53 min.,
   guide, $250. Rental, $75.
   Ages 15–up.

Alex, a high school football star and piano prodigy, is beaten up in a service station restroom for resisting a truck driver's advances. After denying that it was he who "came on" to the truck driver, Alex does confess that he is a homosexual. Alex's parents stand by him, as does his best friend, who even jeopardizes his own relationships and future out of loyalty to Alex. This riveting, exceptionally well-acted adaptation of Anne Snyder's book *Counter Play* (NAL/Signet, 1981) portrays the hostility and misunderstanding gay teens face.

ONE PLUS ONE
MAKES THREE

Baby Blues. National Film Board of
   Canada, 1251 Avenue of the
   Americas, New York, NY 10020.
   1990; released 1991. 24 min.,
   $200. Rental, $50. Ages 14–18.

Jason's thoughts are on playing soccer and Kristen's are on a recently won scholarship until the two are distracted by fears that Kristen may be pregnant. Indeed, the anxiously awaited results of a home pregnancy test confirm their suspicions. Through believable scripting and fine acting, viewers become involved in the young couple's dilemma and are alerted to the necessity of taking sexual responsibility. The film is closed-captioned for the hearing impaired.

Flour Babies. The Media Guild,
   11722 Sorrento Valley Rd.,
   Suite E., San Diego, CA 92121.
   1989; released 1990. 30 min.,
   guide, $345. Ages 13–18.

A high school assignment in which couples must care for a make-believe baby for three weeks gives Donnie and Carrie reason to reconsider their romantic relationship. Prior to this true-to-life responsibility, the couple was considering having sex. Now, alert to the realities of a baby and to the risks of STDs, they communicate respectfully with one another and are able to set a model for postponing sexual activity. This program is a fictional dramatization. *Salt Babies,* described elsewhere in this list, documents the effects of an actual high school family-life class project.

He's No Hero. Intermedia, 1300 Dexter Ave. N, Seattle, WA 98109. 1988. 18 min., guide, $189. Ages 12–18.

The rock music of a racially mixed, teenage band rhythmically underscores a film that deals in an unusual way with male sexual attitudes. Liz, the girlfriend of band leader David, is pregnant. But when she arrives to talk with David about his prospective fatherhood, he is nasty and verbally abusive. Liz and David's situation remains unresolved in the film, but the program's accompanying study guide will facilitate discussion of the weighty issues their drama brings to light.

"I Never Thought It Would Be Like This": Teenagers Speak Out About Being Pregnant/Being Parents. Guidance Associates, Communications Park, Box 3000, Mount Kisco, NY 10549. 1988. 50 min., guide, $209. Ages 12–18.

Clear anatomical diagrams and candid facts about contraception alert teens to the responsibilities that attend their blossoming sexuality. While the production actually encourages viewers to postpone sexual activity, the thoughtful program features three teens who did not. These girls forthrightly share memories of their pregnancies and deliveries and drive home the fact that parenthood is forever. A counselor is also consulted as the program reviews options available for pregnant teens.

Just a Beginning: Pre-Natal Care for Teens. Sunburst Communications, 39 Washington Ave.,
Pleasantville, NY 10570. 1988; released 1991. 22 min., guide, $149. Ages 14–18.

In the first weeks of your pregnancy, look around to find someone you can trust, advises a group of worldly-wise, expectant teenage moms. Their comments and experiences are tied together by the sage remarks of a young, pregnant actress, who looks beyond the immediate needs of pregnant teens to such long-term objectives as staying in or returning to school and achieving pre-baby goals. The invaluable resource also urges pregnant teens to avoid drugs, alcohol, and cigarettes as part of their pre-natal care.

Salt Babies: An Exercise in Teen Parenting. Human Relations Media, 175 Tompkins Ave., Pleasantville, NY 10570. 1990. 15 min., guide, $119. Rental $40. Ages 14–18.

Diapering, dressing, and looking after a five-pound bag of salt for two weeks is the high school health education assignment documented here. As "parents" care for their "babies," their awareness of parental responsibilities is heightened. At the same time, communication about sexual matters is promoted between these teens and their parents.

Teenage Father. Sunburst Communications, 39 Washington Ave., Pleasantville, NY 10570. 1989. 34 min., guide, $199. Ages 13–up.

Spotlighting the young man's point of view, this production introduces three expectant teen couples. Each couple chooses a different way to deal with its unplanned pregnancy: one opts for adoption, another for abortion, and the third has the child out-of-wedlock with the father allowed visitation rights until the mother marries another man. This sensitive, realistic film gives viewers a vicarious opportunity to assess the importance of planned sexual activity.

DEATH: ROMANCE AND REALITY

Empty Chairs. Agency for Instructional Technology, P.O. Box A, Bloomington, IN 47402. 1988. 30 min., guide, $150. Rental, $55. Ages 14–up.

An empty chair on a dark stage symbolizes the place Kate Keily once filled in the lives of those close to her. In compelling monologues, young and talented actors portray teenage Kate's mother, English teacher, boyfriend, sister, best friend, and even Kate, herself. Their reflections on Kate's life and death deftly incorporate the warning signs of suicide and intervention advice while they express survivors' feelings. A moving dramatization of the far-reaching effects and pain of one youngster's suicide.

Friends for Life. Gerald T. Rogers Productions, 5215 Old Orchard Rd., Suite 410, Skokie, IL 60077. 1987. 22 min., $225. Rental, $100. Ages 14–up.

Convincing actors skillfully delivering realistic dialogue engage viewers in five scenarios about suicide and teenage drug and alcohol abuse. The involving vignettes stress the urgency of peer intervention to save the life of a troubled friend. A list of suicide's warning signals concludes the production.

The Power of Choice: Depression and Suicide. Live Wire Video Publishers, 3315 Sacramento St., San Francisco, CA 94118. 1988. 30 min., guide, $64.95. Ages 13–up.

Juvenile probation officer turned stand-up comedian, Michael Pritchard calls on his experiences and his humor to help young adults recognize depression and suicidal symptoms. Pritchard's talent for communicating with teens is equally evident in *The Power of Choice,* a program listed previously, which is aimed at helping teen viewers establish positive goals.

Top Secret: A Friend's Cry for Help. Human Relations Media, 175 Tompkins Ave., Pleasantville, NY 10570. 1989. 27 min., guide, $169. Rental, $40. Ages 13–18.

Karen loves acting and is often on stage, so her close friend Alan can't tell if her confessions of contemplated suicide are legitimate. Because he's unsure of her intentions and because he promised not to tell, Alan is deeply troubled. Should he chance losing Karen's trust at the risk of her life? Though it pauses to let viewers contemplate Alan's dilemma, the sincere yet fresh drama is respectful of *both* teens' problems.

Author-Title Index

Subject Index

Stephanie Zvirin, a former high school teacher and public librarian, joined the staff of the American Library Association in 1976 as a *Booklist* reviewer. A contributing editor to *Best of the Best for Children* (Random, 1992) and a consultant to the American Library Association's Reluctant Young Adult Reader Committee, she is currently Associate Editor, *Booklist* Books for Youth. She lives with her husband, her son, and two rowdy cats in a suburb of Chicago.

After completing her MLS, Ellen Mandel got her feet wet in the library world as a school media specialist. She then joined the *Booklist* staff where, for fourteen years as an assistant editor, she reviewed films, videos, and other audiovisual materials. Now also a licensed pharmacy technician, she divides her time among her husband's corner drugstore, her two young sons, the family dog, and free-lance book and video reviewing.